BOAT OWNER'S GUIDE TO MODERN MAINTENANCE

BOAT OWNER'S GUIDE TO MODERN MAINTENANCE

by John Duffett

W·W·Norton & Company · New York · London

Copyright © 1985 by John Duffett
All rights reserved.
Published simultaneously in Canada by Penguin Books Canada Ltd., 2801
John Street, Markham, Ontario L3R 1B4.
Printed in the United States of America.

The text of this book is composed in Baskerville, with display type set in Baker
Signet. Composition by Com Com Manufacturing by Haddon Craftsmen.
Book design by Bernard Klein.

Library of Congress Cataloging in Publication Data

Duffett, John.
  Boatowner's guide to modern maintenance.

Includes index.
1. Yachts and yachting—Maintenance and repair.
I. Title.
VM331.D83   1983   623.8'208   82-18787

ISBN 0-393-03279-5

W. W. Norton & Company, Inc., 500 Fifth Avenue, New York, N. Y. 10110
W. W. Norton & Company Ltd., 37 Great Russell Street, London WC1B 3NU

Contents

Foreword

It was only seven years ago that my first book, written for boat owners and people whose livelihood is earned around boats, was published by the Hearst Corporation. *Modern Marine Maintenance* had the good fortune to be very well received by its readers. In that volume, for the first time, little-understood materials and techniques that have since become commonplace in the marine industry were explained, evaluated, and gathered together in one convenient reference work. Many of those materials and techniques are now standard in manufacturing the boats of today.

I believe that the most significant development during those seven years has been the emergence of fiberglass-reinforced plastic as the primary material for small-boat hulls. Barring a few exceptions, we have seen metal become increasingly less important as a boatbuilding material.

Because of this development in the technology of construction and changes in the economics of the boating market, I have long felt that a new book was required—one that would lay heavier emphasis on techniques rele-

vant to fiberglass boats. At the same time a new book
would allow me to discuss new developments and new
products that have been created since my last work appeared.

As preparation for this new book I spent a great deal
of time skippering fiberglass boats. It is better to write
of things one knows, and one can only know boats by
sailing them. While in Europe I captained a Bermuda 40
that was built by the prestigious firm of Henry Hinkley
in Southwest Harbor, Maine; in San Diego, California, I
spent much time aboard and working on Herb Johnson's
Vector, a 37-foot fiberglass racing sloop built by Dennis
Choate.

From these two boats, as well as a host of others, many
of the joys and sorrows inherent to fiberglass boats were
added to my experience. Most valuable of all, time
aboard these boats afforded opportunities to make
modifications to, and to work on and maintain, the modern fiberglass-reinforced plastic hull. It is this information that I want to pass on to my readers.

In this work there is new material for the wood-boat
owner as well. Wood boats are still being built in this
country, and the art of wood-boat restoration has become as popular as classic car restoration in the motor
world. This specialty of wood-boat restoration developed many new methods of fabrication. The absence or
scarcity of suitable woods in large scantlings has given
rise to ingenious and practical alternatives to make up
the lack. Wood lamination of large timbers and the Gougeon Brothers' "wood-epoxy saturation technique," by
way of example, are two relatively new solutions to old
problems.

In the years since I first set foot on a yacht's deck I have
seen more fine vessels die from neglect than from wreck.
Great and beautiful Alden Malabar schooners, fine-lined
Lawley and Herreshof sloops—many of them would

swim today if their owners had only realized the uniqueness and irreplaceability of what they had.

It will be the same with today's fiberglass boats. Many of them are pretty examples of the designer's and builder's craft, but they are made of a material that is a by-product of refining petroleum. Perhaps too late we are learning that the supply of resins from petroleum will not last forever. So let us learn and practice the art of keeping what we have alive.

I would like to thank Frank and Brian Casey of Wood Boats, Norwalk, Connecticut, for permitting me to develop some of my theories in their yard, and George Stadel of Stamford, Connecticut, for information on some of the classic wood-boat designs. I also want to thank Svein Molaug, director, and Else Marie Thorstvedt of the Norske Sjø fartsmuseum, Oslo, Norway; the Colin Archer family of Tolderodden, Larvik, Norway; and Ruth Nilsen, owner of *Stavanger*, Rednignshoete #14, who helped me greatly in my investigations into the work and life of Colin Archer. Thanks are in order to Magne Skjaeraasen of the Oslo *Aftenposten* for giving me the opportunity to write about Archer's personal yacht *Mignon*, which by now, I hope, has been saved from oblivion in Spanish waters. Last, I want to thank William Taylor McKeown, one of the great boating editors, who first gave me the opportunity to write about boats and who has been an exemplary shipmate on this gale-swept voyage of life.

J.D.

San Francisco, California
November 1984

BOAT OWNER'S GUIDE TO MODERN MAINTENANCE

1. The Elastomeric Sealants

The biggest problem facing the mariner has always been maintaining the watertight integrity of the hull. Even with monocoque construction, as with fiberglass, it is no small matter to keep buoyancy in and the sea out. Fiberglass is not, as some believe, totally unporous, nor is it immune to certain kinds of deterioration. Wood-boat seams especially, by their nature, give and work and require a versatile caulking. Planking seams are therefore quite vulnerable to penetration by polluted water and marine organisms. Once breakdown of the caulking bond with the seam edges has begun, it proceeds rapidly. Smooth hull surface continuity, produced by seam fillers and luting compounds with good chemical and mechanical adhesion, are of extreme importance to today's boat owner.

One of the most important weapons in the boat owner's arsenal against the ravages of time and the sea is the group of rubberlike compounds known as the "elastomerics." When these compounds first came upon the scene in the early 1950s, they were expensive and not fully understood with respect to proper use. That is no longer the case. Elastomeric products are now competitively priced with other sealants, their proper use is well understood, and their performance over a long period of time has been evaluated.

The formula for elastomeric sealants, according to the folklore of industrial chemistry, was born when a rubber researcher, while attempting to develop a substitute for natural rubber during World War II, was taken with an irrepressible physical need. His solution to that need furnished the missing ingredient—uric acid—to the mixture, and the elastomerics were the result.

These sealants are rubberlike compounds in semiliquid form before cure. When cured, they are elastic, tenacious, and waterproof. They will not dry out and harden over time as will oil-base caulks. The advantage of the synthetic rubber compounds is obvious for wood-boat seams, but what has been less fully realized is their potential for use on fiberglass boats. The elastomerics make an excellent luting compound or bedding between the fiberglass and any material that is fastened to the boat. Between an iron or lead keel and the hull, for example, for bedding hardware to the fiberglass hull, for bedding wood parts to fiberglass, or for setting windows, portlights, or hatches, these sealants are without peer. An added advantage is the ability of the elastomerics—because of their natural resiliency—to "take up the slack" between materials with different coefficients of expansion and contraction. For applications where electric conductors such as grounding plates and wires must be fixed to the hull, or where metals of different electrogalvanic potential are sandwiched, the elastomerics, being nonconductors, make a superior insulating material that can be molded directly in place.

There are several kinds of synthetic rubber com-

pounds in use: those having a polysulfide, a polyurethane, and a silicone base. Water-soluble-before-cure
latex and butyl types are also available but do not lend
themselves to marine use.

The Thiokol Company was the developer of the raw
material used in the various polysulfide formulations.
The name "Thiokol" is often used generically to desig-
nate synthetic rubber compounds having a polysulfide
base. The elastomeric sealants are built of a binder or
base material, together with fillers, plasticizers, additives, and a catalyst. After cure, the sealant becomes a
rubbery mass with roughly the same performance qualities as natural rubber but with greater chemical resistance. All three sealants perform about the same after
cure.

The nature of the curing process marks the difference
between the sealants. The polysulfide compounds cure
by chemical reaction with a catalyst accelerator; the polyurethanes, on the other hand, cure by absorption of
moisture from the ambient atmosphere. Recently, a
polysulfide sealant that cures by moisture absorption has
also been developed in the course of developing a one-
part sealant. As a general rule the polysulfide sealants
cure tack-free in less time than the polyurethanes or
silicones. This makes them better for use where time is
a factor, such as exterior hull or deck seams where extended cure time could be risky. By varying catalyst
input, surface curing time can be adjusted to range from
one hour to one day; in-depth full curing time can be
similarly adjusted.

With a relative humidity of 50 percent and an ambient
temperature of 75° Fahrenheit (24° Celsius), the polyurethanes generally require 24 hours to cure tack-free and
from 7 to 10 days to full cure. Curing time is shortened
as the humidity rises.

RTV (Room-Temperature Vulcanizing)

Silicone-base sealants air-cure without the need for heat, although applied heat will hasten cure. They first form a surface skin, and then cure proceeds throughout the depth of the material. Under typical ambient conditions silicone sealants develop a tack-free surface in 15 to 30 minutes and cure through a ⅛-inch thickness in about 24 hours. Higher temperatures and humidity will hasten the cure. The ideal conditions for use are 90° Fahrenheit (32° Celsius) and 90 percent relative humidity.

Pick Your Curing Time

It is a good idea to allow sufficient working time when choosing an elastomeric sealant for a particular job. If you have only a limited time on the ways or hauled, or if you are charged for extended time on the ways, a faster curing is best. If time is not important, then a slower curing system is adequate.

Two-part packaging was standard for the elastomeric sealants in the past, but this is no longer the case. Polysulfide sealants are manufactured in either one-part or two-part packages. They are also sold in a moisture curing mix, but it is wise to read the label instructions carefully or check with the manufacturer, as this is not always immediately clear. Polyurethane mixtures are generally available in one- or two-part packaging, depending on quantity. Silicone sealants are most popularly sold in one-part tubes or gun cartridges.

Cost Factors

When purchased at marine supply stores, the per-unit cost of all the elastomeric sealants is high. This is not important when a small job is involved as in, say, setting a portlight into a fiberglass hull. But if considerable sealant must be used, as in new construction, cost can be a factor. In this case it is of use to try to find a wholesale distributor who merchandises in large packaging on the order of a gallon or five gallons. One good place to find elastomeric sealants in quantity at workable prices is through a large roofing supply company catering to the construction industry. (Elastomerics are now widely used as bedding and caulking in the roofing trades.) A phone call may result in huge savings. Be sure to discuss the use to which the material will be put with the supplier and ask for enough to run a test application.

Once they are cured, there is little difference in the performance of the systems. Polyurethane, being a one-part system, is easy to use; pot life is long, mixing is unnecessary, no priming of the seams is required. Polyurethane compounds also require considerable curing time and the available colors are limited. Polysulfides come in several colors but require some care in mixing. Pot life is limited, care must be taken that the mixture does not "go off" (catalyze) prematurely, and priming the seams is advisable. The extra care needed with polysulfide is worthwhile as it is the preferred system for old wood or difficult fiberglass applications.

Silicone, when cured, seems to have about the same properties as the others but exhibits superior dielectric strength and resistance to electric current. Adhesion of silicones is not as good as the other sealants. Recommended seam depth, width, and filling must be followed carefully. Because of their lubricity, silicones had a reputation for poor paint coverability, but makers claim to have solved this problem. A paint test of silicone sealants to be used in any prominent location would be advisable, and this holds true for any sealant as well.

BEST WAY TO USE

With a few precautions, failures with the elastomerics are extremely rare. Contamination of seam edges and faying surfaces by oil or petroleum by-products will be likely to cause nonbonding. Care should be taken to keep surfaces free of asphalt, creosote, Woodlife, or Penta. Dry rot or crumbled wood should be chipped out, and grease should be wiped from fiberglass surfaces with lacquer thinners or resin solvent. The sealant can be pressed into seams with a putty knife or forced in with a caulking gun. When filling narrow seams, you can use masking tape to limit the staining of surrounding areas, but the tape should be removed before the compound sets (see Figure 1).

When luting between such wide structural members as double planking, keel and keelson, or between bolted-on additions like keel or rubbing strakes and fiberglass, the compound can be spread on with a trowel, like a serrated-edge linoleum trowel (see Figure 2). Again, it is a good idea to prime before applying polysulfide, no matter where the application.

If the seams to be filled are very deep—as in decking over fiberglass—they should be lightly caulked with untreated cotton to within ½ inch of the surface. In no case should a seam be filled less than ¼ inch in depth. Though elastomerics are extremely tenacious and adhesive, a bonding surface of at least ¼ inch is necessary on each side of the seam for maximum bond.

SPECIAL FORMULAS

Many manufacturers of elastomerics offer different sealant formulas for different job applications. A variety of colors—black, amber, brown, and aluminum are some—and mixtures with different performances are made. For

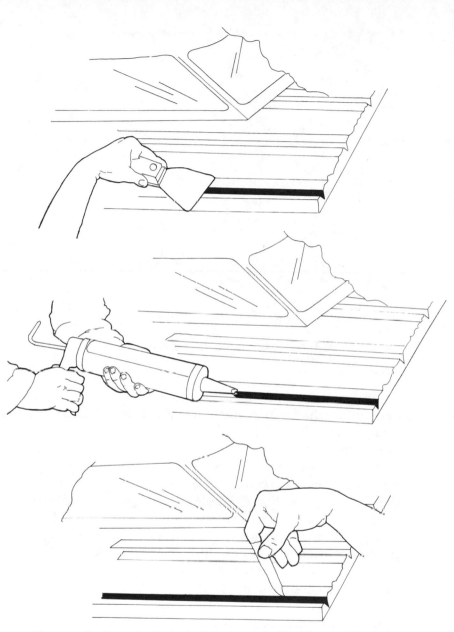

Figure 1. Caulking the Deck. A. *Tape along each side of the seam before forcing sealant in with a caulking gun.* **B.** *Then knife the caulking in with a wide, flexible-bladed putty knife, leaving the caulking flush with the deck.* **C.** *When the sealant is tacky to the touch, peel off the tape. After complete curing the filler sealant should be sanded flush to the deck.*

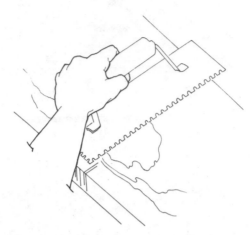

Figure 2. Luting between Wide Structural Members. *When luting between wide structural members such as keel timbers, use a linoleum trowel with a serrated edge to spread the elastomeric.*

filling vertical seams, a formula with a viscosity great enough so that it will not run or sag is available. A semipourable "self-leveling" grade is thinner and facilitates gun application to deck and horizontal seams. In addition to viscosity, the new sealants are available in several grades of cured hardness, measured according to the Shore Index. For example, Shore 70 is about the hardness of an automobile tire; Shore 10 is about like sponge rubber. Most manufacturers sell stock compounds restricted to either hard- or soft-curing kinds. If you anticipate any special or unusual problems, write to the technical department of the particular manufacturer.

MIXING AND EXPERIMENTING

Helpful hints for clean, easy application as well as mixing instructions for the two-part compounds are supplied by the makers. For the one-part compounds, no mixing is necessary. After two-part sealants have been mixed, they can be stored for several days without "going off" (catalyzing), by placing them in a freezer. When thawed to room temperature, they are handled as though freshly mixed.

It is very good procedure, when first using an elastomeric on a new application, to try a small quantity in an area that is not critical. This dry-run test can uncover any bugs in your techniques and prevent failure by premature or delayed curing.

The elastomeric sealants are safe to handle if reasonable precautions are taken. Because some of them contain lead compounds, prolonged contact should be avoided especially where there are open cuts in the skin. Hands should be protected with gloves or a standard industrial protective cream. Before eating or smoking, wash your hands well.

Many of these compounds contain or are thinned with spirits like toluene, methylethylketone, and xylene. Wear an air-supplied respirator where a dangerous concentration of fumes is possible, such as in the forepeak or fo'c'sle. Where ventilation is adequate this is not necessary.

With the new silicones, treatment of electrical connections to provide insulation and protection from corrosion is easy. GE's new RTV silicone rubber adhesive sealant can be applied directly to electrical junction box connections. In its transparent form, the terminals and wiring can be seen right through the sealant but are protected from vibration and corrosion. No premixing is required with silicone RTV, and it air-cures with minimum shrinkage.

CAULKING WITH ELASTOMERICS

After the seams have been properly prepared for caulking (see pages 130–37), the first step is to press or drive in—depending on depth and size of the seam—cotton caulking. When used with modern elastomerics, cotton serves a different function than heretofore. Cotton is desirable with the modern synthetics to fill out the seam under the seam sealant. This is done both to save on rubber compound and to form the kind of seam which affords the rubber maximum adhesion. The elastomerics perform best when the depth of the rubber is about half to two-thirds of the total seam depth. Manufacturers recommend this procedure for best curing of the sealant and also to take most advantage of the elasticity of the material.

When the cotton caulking of the deck, for instance, is completed, you can fill out the rest of the seam with elastomeric compound. Before knifing in the compound, mask the edges of the seam with an easily removed masking tape. This will save a lot of work.

For seams that are vertical or at an angle, where there is a possibility that the filler may sag, use a thicker compound than that used for deck seams and fill the seams with a putty knife rather than a caulking gun. The cartridge-gun method requires a more liquid viscosity and it is nearly impossible to keep this grade from drooping out of a vertical seam.

When knifing in elastomerics, a good procedure is to make a palette from a piece of Masonite or plywood. Use a spatula to take a lump of caulking from the can and deposit it on the palette. If you are using a two-part mixture, now work in the catalyst according to the manufacturer's recommendation. Of course, you are certain that the sealant will "go off" at the proper interval because you have already run a rest under identical working conditions and temperature—remember?

Pick up a thin bead of compound on the tip of a good flexible-bladed putty knife and work it firmly into the seam. Keep enough pressure on the blade so that entrapped air bubbles will be forced out. Holding the blade at an angle to the seam will also help avoid trapping bubbles. Wash tools with solvent frequently so they do not load up with old sealant. When removing sealant from the can, replace the lid immediately to avoid skin formation.

When choosing a sealant, remember that some formulations do not hold paint well, so for seams that will be painted over, run a test or look for a manufacturer's statement that the formulation is meant to be painted over. When knifing in, fill just flush with the planking surface, as the compound has a tendency to rise slightly in cure. After cure, any protruding bead may be cut flush with a very sharp chisel or a single-edge razor blade in a suitable holder. Masking tape along the seams should be removed after the compound has become tacky but before complete hardening.

2. Modern Paint Systems

In my earlier writings about modern boat maintenance I was an innovator in stressing that surface coatings utilizing modern chemistry should be thought of as a compatible component "system." That concept is now firmly established, and boat owners today are furnished on the can of paint they purchase with information infinitely more sophisticated than with older oil-base paints. This is so that information needed to prevent failure of the "system" is available.

The requirements of a superior surface coating are: (1) that the coating effectively protect the boat from weathering and the elements, and slow or prevent water absorption; (2) that the coating be compatible with the material of which the boat is built and not cause deterioration; (3) that the elements of the system—primers, undercoats, thinners, and solvents—be compatible with each other; and (4) that the paints reinforce the corrosion resistance, durability, and adhesion of each other.

SYNTHETICS

The most commonly used paints today are synthetic based, resulting when organic acids are mixed with alcohols to "cross-link," thus chemically forming a new, three-dimensional "monomer." Now, the paints we use on boats have always been chemicals, but we never thought of the old linseed-oil enamels that way. They were just paint. The plastic finishes that began to be seen in marine stores after World War II—paints and varnishes that have taken a quantum leap in sophistication during the past two decades—are chemicals not only in definition but in our consciousness of them. With names like "linear polyurethane" and "silicone copolymer," they conjure up the alchemy of real chemistry.

These paints *are* complex chemicals, and they call for some understanding of their chemistry if you want to get the best from them. The most basic understanding to have from the definition of terms which appears below is that each of these paints is a chemical *system,* and that each system—even among chemically similar types from different manufacturers—is different from every other.

The message here is to choose a paint system—thinner, undercoat, finish coat—that you *know* will be chemically compatible, and then to follow the directions very conscientiously. Paint manufacturers report that 99 percent of the paint failures they hear about from disappointed boat owners are due to foreign chemicals introduced into their carefully concocted paint systems or to lack of attention to directions.

Here, to begin, are some definitions:

Paint: Paint consists of a pigment that imparts body and/or color, along with a "vehicle" or "binder." In addition, a "thinner"—a solvent to make the mixture workable—is added. It is the vehicle or binder that determine what kind of paint "system" you are working with; therefore I will be talking exclusively of the composition of the vehicle.

Molecule: The smallest unit of matter that can exist by itself and retain all properties of the original substance.

Mer: A family name, like Jones or Smith. It is the arbitrary name for the repeating structural unit of a paint-vehicle substance. Two mers is a bimer or dimer; three is a trimer; many mers is a polymer. A mer is generally made up of one or more molecules.

Monomer: One mer—a simple compound, usually containing carbon and of low molecular weight, that can react to form a polymer by combining with itself or with other similar molecules or compounds.

Copolymer: A single paint made by combining two differing polymer resins or oils.

Ester: A substance that, on hydrolysis (reaction with water), yields an acid and an alcohol. The reverse of this, the formation of an ester by reaction of an alcohol and an acid, is called *esterification.*

Polyester: "Many esters," so called because the ester resin is made by simultaneous esterification and polymerization of several different chemicals. Surface coatings (gel coats), lay-up resins for fiberglass, and Dacron are all products made from polyesters.

Curing: A loose term meant to describe the successful completion of the film-forming process. The three kinds of curing that will concern us most are: (1) solvent evaporation, drying from the action of solvent volatiles' escaping into the atmosphere; (2) oxidation, oxygen in the air combining with the resin to tie several molecules together and harden the film; and (3) polymerization, small molecules' joining together and growing to make big molecules of a thick, viscous film of high molecular weight. This is the most important curing dynamic of synthetic resins.

MODERN MARINE SURFACE COATINGS AND THEIR CHARACTERISTICS

In discussing paints, generic characteristics can be stated only in broadly general germs. This is because formulas of different manufacturers within the industry vary widely. To say, therefore, that one kind of paint is always "harder" than another mght not always be the case. By way of example, one manufacturer's alkyd could be harder than another's urethane if the latter had been greatly modified with additives. However, in general, the analysis of characteristics made below holds good.

Alkyd-Oil
These paints are made with a binder of synthetic resin obtained by reacting an alcohol such as glycerine or pentaerytritol with phthalic acid in the presence of water. Vegetable-oil-modified alkyd-resin paints are widely used becaue of their relatively low cost and because of the ease with which they can be coupled with phenolics, silicones, and acrylics to achieve different results.

For working convenience and avoidance of failure, alkyd paints are best applied in optimum conditions of 75°–80° ambient temperature and a relative humidity of 50 percent. (These figures, by the way, hold true for most paints.) Paint formulations can be successfully applied within parameters that vary widely from this optimum—experience is the determinant—but it is always best to aim for the optimum conditions.

Alkyd paints are sold ready-mixed in single containers. Curing is by solvent evaporation, oxidation, and polymerization. Alkyds are good paints considering their low cost per gallon—about $20. They excel where the substrate cannot be meticulously prepared, and they are forgiving of minor goofs in application. As a surface they tend to be softer than the epoxies. Their chemical resistance, abrasion resistance, adhesion, flexibility, and gloss retention are fair compared with the new wonder paints. Oil-alkyds are quick-drying and suitable for topsides, decks, and cabins on wood, fiberglass, steel, and aluminum boats.

Resin-Modified Alkyds

Alkyd paints are mixed with other polymerizing resins with the objective of changing the characteristics of the paint binder to obtain different results. Such two-resin paints are referred to as "copolymers."

Phenolic Alkyd

The alkyd is modified with phenols and aldehyes with intent to add hardness to the alkyd coating. Curing is by heat or change of pH, or both. This mixture makes a good deck coating, although it is not as hard or durable as epoxy. The phenolic copolymer uses relatively low-cost chemicals, permitting moderate cost. Phenolic alkyd paints sell at about $25 per gallon.

Silicone Alkyd

Alkyd with silicone, or vice versa, is commonly known as "silicone copolymer." Silicones give the paint added gloss retention, chemical resistance, enhanced color retention, and especially superior heat resistance. The paint dries by solvent evaporation, oxidation, and polymerization. Silicone copolymers are somewhat less easy to apply than alkyds modified with oils or resins, but not difficult if you follow instructions. They retail for about $30 per gallon and are excellent for topsides, cabins, and engine room use.

Acrylic Alkyd

Acrylic is the material known as Plexiglas or Lucite. It is a methyl-methacrylate polymer that is dissolved in the paint. Acrylics cure mainly by solvent evaporation and add surface hardness and gloss retention to a paint. Color retention is enhanced too, since acrylics do not oxidize. This paint is easy to apply and its cost is moderate—about $25 per gallon.

Polyester

Polyester resin is the major building material of the fiberglass-reinforced plastic boat business. It is used in the layup of hulls and for finish gel coating. No significant commercially available surface coating is made of polyester with the exception of gel-coat touch-up. These are usually available from the boat's manufacturer. Polyesters have limited pot life and are difficult to apply, which accounts for their limited use in paint.

Polyurethane Paints

The most dramatic recent development in surface coating for yachts is in the perfection of the urethanes. From a relatively difficult material little used in coatings a few years ago, urethanes have taken off spectacularly. Urethanes are formed from isocyanates and hydroxyls. In modern formulations they are extremely versatile, ranging in properties from extremely hard to flexible. Urethanes are available in two-part (two-can) systems and in slightly modified one-can packages. Urethane systems cure by reactive cross-linking and by absorption of moisture in the prepolymer component of the resin. In the aromatic urethanes, drying is by solvent evaporation as well.

Urethanes have great adhesion, superior hardness and scuff resistance, good gloss and color retention. In white enamels they also resist yellowing. Most urethanes have an ultraviolet-resistant chemical added to counteract their tendency to deteriorate under sunlight. This additive is so effective that polyurethane paints are recommended for use in tropical as well as temperate climates.

Urethane paints require care in application. Manufacturers' recommendations for mixing of the two-can systems should be carefully followed. Application in direct sunlight can cause set-up so quickly that brush marks do not have time to level out. Use of less catalyst for slower drying can result in sagging and dust-impregnation of the coating. As with all painting, try for a shaded, warm, dust-free environment for best results. Urethane paints are more expensive than alkyds; single-can systems sell in the $25-per-gallon range, and two-can systems go for $45–$60 per gallon. Higher cost is generally offset by greater longevity. When using urethanes, *carefully read the label and any other instructions you can lay hands on!*

Epoxy Paints
Epoxies are formed by the reaction of hydroxyls and amines. At one time epoxies were thought to hold promise of being the outstanding marine paint. However, improvement in formulation of the urethanes, with their greater ease of application, seems to have displaced epoxies. Epoxy systems, on the other hand, are still outstanding for application to steel hulls, where adhesion is always a problem. Epoxies make a chemical as well as a mechanical bond with steel. When properly applied they have excellent hardness, high gloss, and resistance to abrasion and chemical attack.

For topside paint, epoxies tend to chalk; their gloss retention is not good and they are ultraviolet-degradable. Recoatability is only fair. Two-can systems, because of high viscosity, are not noted for ease of application. Two-can systems sell for about $35 per gallon and one-can epoxy copolymer formulations for about $25. Epoxy copolymers—with ester resins added—are offered by some manufacturers in antifouling bottom coats, which work well.

Vinyl Paints
There are some dozens of raw materials that can result in vinyl and vinyl-type resins. Most in one form or another are based on the polyvinylchloride long-chain linear molecule. Vinyls cure by oxidation and cross-linking polymerization. Basic formulations can be modified with many different chemicals to obtain differing results. For boat use, the major importance of the vinyls is as a vehicle for antifouling substances such as copper-oxide or the several toxic tin compounds recommended for antifouling protection of aluminum. Vinyls act somewhat like rubber in that they are extremely flexible. They cure quickly, and have good intercoat adhesion and superior chemical resistance. Vinyls are sometimes demanding to apply, however. The strong solvents used in their formulation can lift off previous coatings if the maker's recommendations are not followed. Vinyl antifouling paints are priced proportionately with the amount of active ingredient in the vehicle, but sell for around $68–$72 per gallon. Those toxic metals that make an antifouling finish work are expensive chemicals.

Chlorinated Synthetic Rubber
This is one of the newer antifouling paints now avilable for fiberglass and metal hulls. Chemically they are based on the butadiene-styrene copolymer. The films dry quickly by solvent evaporation and some oxidation cross-linking. The coats dry quickly to a very hard con-

sistency. Unlike vinyls, the solvents are mild and lift-off is not a problem. And their toxic antifouling properties are not affected by being out of water, which makes the chlorinated rubber antifoulings a superior choice for boats that are trailered or stored ashore between races. Cost is proportionate to the amount of active ingredient in the formulation, with pure TBTF going for about $52 and cuprous-oxide with TBTF at about $93. Application is straightforward, but follow the maker's instructions. The high intial cost of these paints is thought to pay off in greater longevity.

WHAT'S IN THE CAN?

The way to use any surface-coating system successfully is to *read the damn can!* At one time this didn't mean much, because manufacturers outdid one another in mystification or outright omission of content descriptions.

Recent legislation by the Environmental Protection Administration requires that any paint containing toxic substances have all its components listed on the label. In addition, many states, such as Virginia, require that *all* paint be fully labeled as to ingredients. Rather than produce separate packagings for different states, manufacturers are now labeling all their products with full descriptions. If you find a can that isn't so labeled—don't buy it. If you find one that is labeled with full ingredients and instructions, buy it and then study the label a while. The information on the can won't guarantee that you do perfect work, but it should guarantee that the paint will perform to specifications.

Modern chemistry and compounds have not changed the two basic rules for successful painting: (1) always start with a clean and properly prepared surface; (2) always read and follow the directions on the can.

PAINTING PRINCIPLES

- Read the instructions on the can.
- Clean and prepare the surface carefully.
- Remove loose flakes of the previous coat, and all of it if you are in doubt about its compatibility with the new paint.
- Use the same brands, if possible, for each coat.
- Observe specified temperature and humidity requirements.
- Note if the boat should be launched while the bottom paint is still wet.
- Clean all brushes before they dry.

WHAT PAINT FOR WHAT SURFACE?

Aluminum

Your boat builder can probably recommend the proper paints and tell you which brands were previously used. Vinyl-base paints are usually satisfactory. Prepare previously unpainted aluminum by washing with an etching cleaner. Then rinse and let dry before applying vinyl-base primer.

Before applying antifouling bottom paint, start with vinyl primer-undercoater. Final coats should be vinyl base with tributyl tin oxide as the active toxic agent, called TBTO or Bio-Met. Use of copper or red-lead paints is not recommended.

Canvas

Paint coats year after year on canvas decks can build up layers that accelerate cracking. One answer is to use low-cost house paint that chalks and wears off during the season. Synthetic resin paints are also suitable, and sand or a grit compound can be added to the final coat for a nonskid surface.

Treat flexible canvas tops and covers with primer and one of the new liquid vinyl coatings.

Engines
Paints that resist high heat are used, and fire-retardant paints or additives can be employed to paint the engine compartment.

Fiberglass
An unpainted surface should first be washed with solvent to remove any wax or mold-release substance. Cracks, dents, or orange-peel hairlines can be filled with a surfacing compound recommended by the paint manufacturer. Alkyd, alkyd acrilic, alkyd polyurethane, polyurethane, polyester silicone, epoxy, and vinyl paints are all satisfactory for use on fiberglass.

Tinted epoxy and polyester resins are now available with pigments to match breaks in the gel coat or areas that have weathered and changed color so that molded-in hue can be matched.

Boats that are hauled out after every use may need no bottom paint, but could use a hard gloss containing no antifouling properties for speed.

For antifouling treatment, no primer may be needed after the solvent wash to remove any wax. Copper-, lead-, or tin-bearing antifouling paints may be used with any base except the alkyds.

Lower Drive Units
Stern drive and outboard motor shafts that stick down into the water may be treated with anticorrosive enamels, and in some cases with antifouling compounds. Engine builders and paint manufacturers can make recommendations. Original colors can usually be matched.

Steel
Once the metal has been properly prepared, paints used on wood, fiberglass, or aluminum, as well as those with special rust inhibitors, can be employed. First, sandblast or use an etching-type wash. Then prime with zinc chro-

mate, red lead, or another rust inhibitor.

Before applying antifouling paint on the bottom, two coats of barrier nonmetallic paint should go over the primer beneath the final antifouling. Galvanic corrosion could resut if copper-bearing paint comes in contact with the steel. Some paint producers provide a system of compatible paints for steel-hull use.

Vinyl

Cushions, seat covers, and curtains as well as tops and cockpit covers of vinyl can be renewed with liquid vinyl coatings available in many colors.

Wood

Alkyd, alkyd acrilic, alkyd polyurethane, polyurethane, polyester silicone, epoxy, latex liquid rubber, and vinyl are suitable for application on wood. Success, however, will depend on how well the wood surface has been cleaned, sanded, and prepared. Primers and fillers should usually be of the nonoily type, and preferably of the same brand as the final paint. A wood bottom may be treated with any of the antifouling paints or with a hard, nontoxic racing surface if the boat will not be left in the water.

Varnishes, whether tung oil and phenolic resin types or the newer synthetics and two-part epoxy systems, require careful application. Follow instructions as to surface sanding and bleaching if brightwork has weathered. Then, on a nearly windless day with the right temperature, apply the number of coats recommended.

How Much Paint Do You Need?*

In estimating the amount of material needed for a specific job, you may assume that one gallon of paint or

*From the Woolsey booklet *How to Paint Your Boat,* copyright © 1967 by Woolsey Marine Industries, Inc. Reprinted by permission.

enamel will cover 500 square feet for one coat on the average painted surface. Over new wood, figure 325 square feet per gallon. One gallon of varnish will cover 750 square feet average on recoat work, and 500 square feet on new wood. Paint and varnish remover may take several applications and consequently can be expected to soften only about 200–250 square feet per gallon.

Some Useful Formulas

Here are some formulas based on practical experience. They should help you determine how much paint you will need. The results are stated in gallons.

Spars (Varnished)

Multiply the greatest diameter (in feet) by the length (in feet), and multiply the result by 2.5. For new wood, divide the result by 500 and for previously finished wood divide by 750 to obtain the gallonage required.

For example, suppose you have a new spar 8 inches in diameter and 40 feet long. Then $[(8/12) \times 40 \times 2.5]/500 = {}^{67}/_{500}$ or approximately ⅛ gallon (1 pint) for the priming coat. For refinishing work a pint is enough for about 1½ coats. To determine the requirements for painted spars, change the coverage factor to 325 for new work and to 500 for previously painted wood.

Cabins or Deckhouses

Multiply the height of the deckhouse (in feet) by the girth (in feet). Deduct the area of any large spaces such as windows and doors. If the deckhouse is to be painted, divide the result by 325 for the priming coat and 500 for each finishing coat. If it is to be varnished, divide by 500 for the first coat and 750 for the following coats.

Decks

Multiply the length of the boat (in feet) by its greatest beam (in feet) and then multiply the result by 0.75. From this, deduct the area of cabin houses, hatches, and so on. Divide the remainder by 325 to obtain gallons required for priming coat and by 500 for each finishing coat of color.

If the deck is to be coated with varnish, divide the figure by 500 and 750, respectively.

Topsides

Multiply the length overall (in feet) by the greatest freeboard (in feet), then multiply the result by 1.5. Divide by 325 for new work and by 500 for old work to obtain the necessary gallonage.

The Bottom

Multiply the waterline length by the draft (in feet). For a keel boat multiply the result by 3.5, and for a centerboard boat multiply the result by 300 for priming new work and by 400 for subsequent coats to get the required gallonage.

Table 1
Estimates of Average Paint Requirements for Two Coats over Existing Finish[a]

SIZE	Topside	Bottom	Boottop	Deck	Varnish	Flybridge	Interior	Engine
10' Dinghy	1 qt.	1 pt.	—	—	1 qt.	—	—	—
14' Rowboat	2 qts.	1 qt.	—	—	—	—	—	—
14' Outboard	1 qt.	1 qt.	½ pt.	1 pt.	1 qt.	—	—	Single aerosol
18' Runabout	1 qt.	3 qts.	½ pt.	1 qt.	1 qt.	—	—	Single aerosol
20' Sailboat	2 qts.	3 qts.	½ pt.	3 qts.	2 qts.	—	—	—
24' Runabout	2 qts.	3 qts.	½ pt.	1½ qts.	2 qts.	—	—	Single aerosol
24' Utility	2 qts.	3 qts.	½ pt.	1½ qts.	1 qt.	—	—	Single aerosol
25' Cruiser	3 qts.	3 qts.	1 pt.	2 qts.	2 qts.	—	2 qts.	Single aerosol
32' Cruiser	2 gals.	1½ gals.	1 pt.	2 qts.	3 qts.	1 pt.	2 qts.	2[b] aerosols
36' Sailboat	2 gals.	2 gals.	1 pt.	1 gal.	1 gal.	—	3 qts.	Single aerosol
40' Cruiser	2½ gals.	2 gals.	1 pt.	1½ gals.	1 gal.	1 qt.	1 gal.	2[b] aerosols
60' Yacht	4 gals.	5 gals.	1 qt.	3½ gals.	2½ gals.	2 qts.	2½ gals.	4[b] aerosols

[a]Over *bare wood* quantities shown will be about double. Less will be required on fiberglass or metal.
[b]Requirements for twin-engine installation. Halve quantities for single engine.

PAINT LOG for . . .

Surface	Color	Product Used	Amount	Cost	Amount	Cost	Amount	Cost
Spars								
Decks								
Brightwork								
Cabins								
Interior								
Topsides								
Boot topping								
Bottom								
Engine								
Dinghy								
Seams								

3. Proper Cleaning— Primary Maintenance for the Fiberglass Boat

The most important principle in achieving low upkeep and long life in fiberglass (FRP) boats is to maintain the integrity of the gel coat. In fiberglass construction the gel coat is the barrier that prevents abrasion or chemical action from deteriorating the underlying laminates.

In this view it is extremely important that the gel coat be protected from breakdown or wearing through. If the integrity of the gel coat is breached, then the whole "system" of fiberglass construction and its claim to low maintenance and long life is sacrificed.

Proper and frequent cleaning, protection from abrasion and sun, and prompt repair of minor nicks and gouges are necessary to assure gel coat life. Probably the most important of these is regular cleaning. When particles of grit or sand fall on the gel coat, walking on the surface or rubbing along a dock, even when well fendered, will scratch the boundary layer of the coating. In time large areas of the gel coat will have been minutely opened to penetration by ozone, ultraviolet rays, and water vapor. If the condition is permitted to continue for long periods, a deterioration of the laminates under the gel coat will take place. A clue that this is happening will be the familiar discolored and lusterless outer layer of synthetic resin.

To remedy this situation, wash the hull thoroughly with soap and warm water, rinse well, and then restore the luster with one of the many marine fiberglass cleaner/polishes (see Figure 3). Specialized products for this purpose are made by many companies and some are listed at the end of this chapter. For most boats this polishing will restore the luster, and a wax coating can then be applied to seal off the finish from chemical or vapor penetration. The most favored wax coating formula at this time would seem to be one of the new carnauba formulas which apply easily and buff to a fairly hard, protective coating.

If polishing is not sufficient to remove chalking, then the fiberglass finish usually requires use of a stronger cleaner that acts by removing a tiny bit of the pigment-containing gel coat. These compounds are mildly abrasive, and are similar to the rubbing compound used on automobile finishes. Kuhls and Dupont are among the companies that make such special paste rubbing compounds. Stains and minor scratches should come out with a household cleanser such as Ajax or a very light rubbing with #600-grit, wet-or-dry sandpaper, after which a cleaner should be applied, followed by a waxing and buffing.

After any rubbing of the surface, a coating of carnauba wax designed for fiberglass should be applied. This will protect the finish from further discoloration due to sunlight—the bane of synthetics—and further chalking. The wax can be buffed with a soft, dry cloth, or with a lambswool pad on a disc sander or electric drill. (see Figure 3C). When buffing, be careful not to cut through the gel

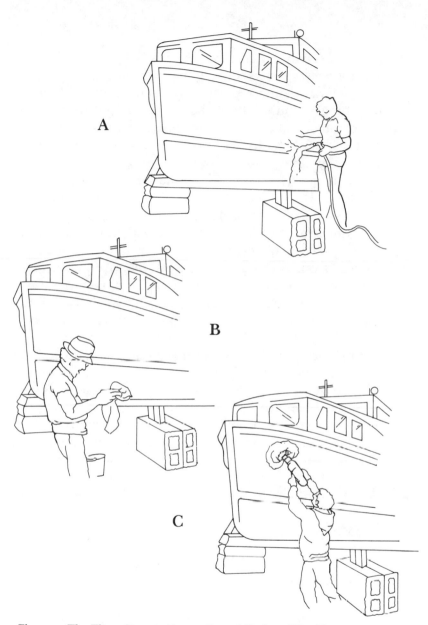

Figure 3. The Three Steps to Ensure Long Life for a Fiberglass Boat. A. *Rinse the fiberglass frequently by hosing with a strong stream of fresh water.* **B.** *Then wash thoroughly with detergent and warm water, and rinse again.* **C.** *Finally, wax with a carnauba wax and buff lightly with a power polisher. Incidentally, the same procedures will ensure longer life for wood-boat surface finish as well.*

coat, especially on corners and edges.

If there is crazing—small gouges or cracking caused by hull flexing—some repair work will have to be done to the fiberglass hull, followed by refinishing. If the gouges are extensive, that is, if they penetrate through the gel coat and have badly damaged the reinforcing glass fibers, then a patch will have to be put in. Manufacturers of patching kits such as Fiber-Glass-Evercoat Co., Petit Paint Co., H. B. Fred Kuhls Co., Travaco Labs, and Sav-Cote Chemical Labs package these kits with detailed instructions for their use. For tinier dents and crazing in gel coat, a small portion of matching gel coat can be secured from your marine dealer and applied according to the directions. No matter how hard you try, it is impossible to match gel coat touch-up exactly—there will always be a slight color difference. For deeper nicks, scratches, and gouges just through the gel coat, the procedure is simple. If the boat is to be repainted, the indentations can be putty-knifed level with an epoxy or polyester putty-type patching compound. When dry, this can be sanded smooth with the hull.

Before applying any gel coat or patching compound to the repair area, first remove the mold-release agent and any wax that might be there with a dewaxer solution obtainable from the same manufacturers that produce the patching kits.

How to Clean

There are a number of new and old products and techniques that will help in cleaning and I will discuss some of them here.

A thorough scrubdown gives you a chance to study the boat and note fittings that are worn, fastenings that need replacement, and any orange telltale signs of rust weeping out from below the surface. Start your renewal and replacement checklist as the work progresses.

Basic Clean-up Kit

- 50 feet of hose
- Soap and scouring cleanser
- Rust remover and old rags
- Large sponge and long-handled mop
- Bilge cleaner compound
- Metal polish and wax
- Scouring pads, steel or bronze wool
- Wet-or-dry sandpaper
- Rubber gloves

Keep a small selected kit of these things aboard.

Topsides
With all covers and bracing removed, first hose down the topsides to wash off all traces of salt, dust, and loose grime. Scrub with a trisodium-phosphate–base cleaner, available from paint, hardware, and building supply outlets. Stubborn spots can be treated with scouring powder, although this may remove gloss. Areas dulled by scouring must be buffed to renew gloss.

Bottom
Growth, scum, and waterline weeds along the boot topping that were not removed when the boat was hauled have now hardened and are twice as hard to get off. Local marine stores may stock compounds particularly suitable for loosening the dirt. As with bottom paints, your most effective mix may vary from harbor to harbor.

• Hose the bottom to wash off or soften any growths.
• Attack barnacles with a metal scraper.
• Use a power sander on stubborn spots.
• Keep wetting the bottom to avoid breathing toxic dust if antifouling paint has been used.
• Note seams or gouges that will require sealant or pointing up before painting.
• Recall and note down, if possible, the brand of bottom paint previously used. Application of a new type may not bond to the old formulation. If in doubt, cleaning down to the bare hull may be necessary.

Bilge

Hose out and pump out bilges, checking the free flow of limber holes and the functioning of the pumps at the same time. Rewash with bilge cleaner compound or soap concentrate.

If your boat normally has some rainwater, spray, or leakage collecting in the bilge, consider one of the bilge-cleaner additives that slosh around and maintain a clean condition whle the boat is under way. If the boat is hauled, remove the drain plugs and scrub the bilges with a strong trisodium-phosphate solution.

Engines

Use a marine or automotive cleaner such as "Gunk" that can degrease and remove caked dirt from the engine so that the condition of the paint, excessive rusting, chafing hoses, or loose control linkage can be observed. Run automotive solvent through the carburetor to dissolve any gum formation. Add water-inhibitor to the gas tanks as well.

Interiors

• Wash down the bulkheads with soap and water, or a cleaner such as Nautabrite.

- Aboard wood boats, treat the forepeak and cuddy corners that get little ventilation with anti-dry-rot compounds.
- After washing and airing, use one of the fungus-control treatments like MRD Mildew and Anti-Rot Spray to inhibit must and mold in cabinets and lockers.

Lines

Give all cordage a freshwater washing while examining them for chafe. Switch end-for-end to equalize wear, and replace if in doubt. Spotcheck by untwisting lay to examine for interior sand that could be chafing the line. Do not use a pressure hose in washing since this also might force in cutting grit.

Metals

Aluminum: Remove oil and grease with cleaning fluid. A cleaner-wax-polish combination will treat bare aluminum. For painted aluminum, use mild soap and water or auto-body-paint polish-cleaner.

Brass, Bronze, Chrome: Regular metal cleaners and polishes will remove tarnish. Use a heavy-duty compound like ABC Metal Cleanser for tougher corrosion. Spray coating or waxes will help metals keep their shine.

Stainless, Iron, Monel: Scouring pads and powder can remove surface rust. Use products like Rust-Away or Naval Jelly for extensive rust. Polish with a wire brush. Rinse down and wax.

Plastics

Fiberglass, Formica, Royalite: Various products are now sold specifically for fiberglass cleaning. (See the list at the end of this chapter.) Gel coat stains can be scoured, though buffing afterward with a product like DuPont White Compound may be necessary to renew gloss plus matching color. Wax for fiberglass can protect the surface. (See the list at the end of this chapter.)

Plexiglas: Use mild soap and water but no scouring powder. Salt crystals can be washed off with a compound like Travaco's Sea—2 Liquid Concentrate. This also works as wash fluid with windshield wipers. Scratches can be removed with special buffing compounds.

PVC (Polyvinyl Chloride): Wood alcohol can be used sparingly, but will soften the surface if overdone.

Sails

Coastal sailors should have washed out salt when the sailboat was hauled. Mild sudsing with soap (no detergents) plus a freshwater rinse is the best spring treatment. (See the list at the end of this chapter.)

Wood

Painted Surfaces: Washing down with a cleaning fluid like Soilax is sufficient. For cabinets, mix in an antifungus additive.

Varnished Surfaces: Wash down. Breaks in the varnish surface of mahogany may have allowed discoloration to start and will require bleaching before revarnishing.

Teak: Use one of the special teak cleaners. Then restore color with a compound. (See the list at the end of the chapter.)

MANUFACTURERS AND SUPPLIERS OF SPECIALIZED CLEANERS AND POLISHES FOR FIBERGLASS BOATS

James Bliss & Co., Route 128, Dedham, MA 02026.
    Cleaners, polishes.
Boat Life Inc., 5–45 49th Ave., Long Island City, NY 11101.
    Complete line of polishes, FRP carnauba wax, bilge cleaners, stainless scrubbers, and elastomeric sealants.

Boater's Choice, 23783 SW 133rd Ave., Miami, FL 33170.

Exceptional line of polishes, cleaners, stain removers, waxes for FRP boats.

Davis Instruments, P.O. Box 3157, San Leandro, CA 94578.

Special foaming sail cleaner, sail bleach, sail bath.

Fiberglas Evercoat, 6800 Cornell Rd., Cincinnati, OH 45242.

Patching kits, resins, polycel foam sealant, cleaners.

International Paint Co., 21 West St., New York, NY 10006.

Paints plus cleaners, polishes, solvents for fiberglass.

Johnson Wax, 1525 Howe St., Racine, WI 53400.

Cleaners, polishes, and waxes for FRP.

Kiekhaefer Mercury, 1939 Pioneer Rd., Fond du Lac, WI 54935.

Specialized cleaning products for fiberglass boats.

Marine Development and Research Corp., 116 Church St., Freeport, NY 11520 (tel. 516/546-1162).

This company sells "Mold-Away" to kill and prevent mold and "Marine Mildew Spray," a boon to sailors. Send for their catalog.

Petit Paint Co., 507 Main St., Belleville, NJ 08742.

Cleaners, polishes, paints.

Star Brite Inc., P.O. Box 300, Coral Gables, FL 33134.

A complete line of the latest developments in fiberglass cleaners, polishes, and waxes, including stain removers and vinyl protectants.

Sudbury Laboratories, 572 Dutton Rd., Sudbury, MA 01776.

Cleaners, polishes, bilge cleaners, holding tank chemicals.

Travaco Laboratories, Inc., 345 Eastern Ave., Chelsea, MA 02150.

Wide range of cleaners, solvents, and fiberglass repair kits.

Woolsey Marine Industries, Inc., 201 East 42nd St., New York, NY 10017.

Solvents, cleaners, polishes for FRP.

4. Typical Fiberglass Boat Construction

Fiberglass (FRP) is an excellent boatbuilding material. Experience and time have amply proven its worth. Provided your boat has been designed by a competent naval architect, put into production by a reputable manufacturer, and built by honest craftsmen, it will afford you years of pleasure and trouble-free ownership. If purchased used and properly cared for, an FRP boat represents a prudent investment.

In order better to learn how to care for your boat, it is well to understand the building techniques involved in FRP construction. As a boatbuilding material FRP stands up well in the marine environment and can endure severe impact without distortion or rupture. Because little water is absorbed into the skin and because the smooth nature of the material permits the boundary layer of water to flow with little turbulence, FRP makes for a fast hull.

The costs of upkeep when fitting-out and decommissioning are greatly reduced over other materials. No material, including fiberglass, is "maintenance free" no matter how creative the advertising writers become. To keep the original structural integrity of a boat, internal bulkheads and longitudinal partitions must be kept in good shape, as these members are often the major means of holding the hull rigid. Good practice in storing and shoring the boat on land is essential to keeping the shape true. Proper cleaning and protection of the surface is necessary to prevent breakdown of the gel coat and laminations. Because the direct rays of the sun are especially destructive to FRP, it is worthwhile to keep the boat covered when out of commission and to use a polish that has an ultraviolet-filtering effect when in use.

It is easier to obtain financing for fiberglass boats, they usually have better insurance rates, and they tend to hold their value on the used-boat market better than craft built of other materials.

On the minus side, fiberglass is not a warm material like wood. It is often cold, unaesthetic, and noisy. Under some conditions moisture can condense on the inside of the hull, making living below unpleasant. Unless generously sound insulated, the monocoque construction sometimes causes the FRP boat to have sound-transmitting characteristics such that one feels like one is living inside a hollow drum. Installing sound-insulating materials and vapor barriers can modify these negative characteristics. Generous use of wood trim and planning for proper stowage can greatly overcome objectionable sound transmission to almost equal the effect of living aboard a wood boat.

In summary, fiberglass is a superior boatbuilding material. Learning to work with it and to maintain it should be the goal of every fiberglass-boat owner. A look at the way FRP hulls are constructed will give the boat owner a better tool for basic fiberglass-boat maintenance.

It is useful to draw an analogy with cement construction. Portland cement, as is well known, has little inherent strength. On the other hand when concrete is poured over a reinforcing rod or screen mesh and allowed to cure, the two materials exhibit a synergistic effect. Ferrocement—a material of greater strength in combination than the combined effect of either material used separately—is the result. This same principle applies to fiberglass-reinforced plastic (FRP).

To build a hull, fiberglass cloth is encased in layers of liquid resin. When the resin cures, a hard, smooth, semielastic shell is formed that has characteristics ideal for boats. The equivalent to the screen or rod mesh in concrete construction is a reinforcing of spun or extruded glass filaments that are formed into threads. The threads are then made into cloth or loosely criss-crossed to form "woven roving." Threads can also be chopped into short segments of varying size and blown, along with liquid resin, onto a previously prepared surface. Filaments can have a light binder added and be compressed into a "mat" somewhat like felt. All of these techniques are found frequently in construction of the modern boat.

HAND LAY-UP MOLDING

With hand lay-up construction, a female "mold" or a male "plug" is prepared to receive the laminates of glass and liquid resin. The mold is smoothed and coated with a mold-release agent having a wax base. This agent allows ready release of the cured shell without sticking. A super-smooth coating of a special resin called a "gel coat" is then sprayed over the release agent. The gel coat usually contains mixed-in pigment to form the final finish color of the hull. A layer of fiberglass cloth is next draped and smoothed over the gel coat and a layer of resin is flowed on and squeegeed smooth also. Alternating layers of woven roving or glass mat are positioned and saturated with resin until the designed thickness is reached.

Requirements for bulking out to a given thickness and the specified structural strength determine how much woven roving or mat is used. Woven roving has great strength along the longitudinal direction of the fibers but a "waffle" effect is left after cure by its coarse weave. To hide this coarseness, mat is generally laid on and saturated with resin. Finally, the hull interior is finished with a layer of finer weave cloth for both strength and smoothness. Between each of the laminates resin is flowed on. It is *how* the resin is applied that determines the quality of the hull. The goal in hand lay-up application of resin is to attain complete and uniform saturation of the reinforcing material without incurring any areas of excess resin deposit. A condition called "resin richness" exists when too much resin localizes at a given area. Under torsional stress and tension, an excess of resin without reinforcement of glass fiber tends to develop radial cracks called "crazing," which are similar to the "alligatoring" of poor or thickly applied paint. Crazing breaks down the surface of laminate and causes it to become brittle. Extensive crazing can cause local failure of the laminate and destroy the watertightness of the hull.

At the other extreme, care must also be taken when building up laminates so that there is complete saturation and no "resin poor" areas develop. Starved of resin, reinforced fiberglass can bubble, lift, and delaminate. Resin-starved patches on a hull can be detected by the sound when struck with a hammer. The difference in sound between a good, solid laminate and a poor one is given away by the "hollow thump" of starved laminate as opposed to the crisp "ringing" of good laminate. Raised bubbles are also a sure sign of a section skipped when resin was flowed on.

The skill and care with which workers apply resin is the main factor in achieving good quality in hand lay-up construction. Most major boatbuilders have tricks and wrinkles to ensure good resin saturation. Don't fail to take advantage of any opportunity to visit the factory or yard of any local boatbuilder to become familiar with some of these construction techniques.

One thing to look for in fiberglass boats is increased reinforcement in the way of major structural sections. Where hardware is attached, at the bow, at the transom and sheer, or in the way of engine beds or propeller and rudder fittings, there should be a considerable addition to the number of roving or mat laminates. These extra laminates should be smoothly blended into the hull. An inspection here is a good method of evaluating craftsmanship throughout.

Core Construction
With hand lay-up building, other materials are employed to bulk, stiffen, and strengthen the construction. Often this is accomplished by the insertion of a core or "sandwich" between the layers of glass. Material used for this purpose may be plywood, balsa-wood blocks, honeycomb fiberglass, honeycomb cardboard, preformed fiberglass stringers, or polyurethene foam. Where considerable compression strain is encountered or where sound deadening is desired, balsa wood and plywood are both used. Transoms that must support an outboard motor, cabin tops, decks, cockpits, and cabin soles frequently have wooden cores. A honeycomb of plastic and fiberglass is usually specified in the hull above the waterline and wherever panels require stiffening without an increase in the weight-to-strength ratio. Where large panels, such as in the bottom of boats, must be stiffened against flexing, "top hat" (all names refer to their appearance), "I-beam," and "Tee" preformed fiberglass members are used as longitudinal stringers.

Such component members as these are generally

made by extrusion, vacuum injection, or die molding. Cementing with resin and a cloth laminate overlay is used to attach the stringers to the skin. Hulls having large-area panels in the bottom or topsides that flex with varying water pressure—as in runabouts, fishermen, or cruisers with hard-chine design—sometimes suffer stringer failure if they are not well bonded. Owners should check this area from time to time to make certain there is no beginning of delamination from stress or other incipient failure. If any weak spots are discovered, additional stiffening may be added as outlined in Chapter 6.

Formed-in-place urethanes or fitted urethane foam blocks provide another method of adding buoyancy, stiffening, and thickness. Because structural strength of urethane foam is low, its primary function is buoyancy. Urethanes come in a two-part system, which is mixed in a liquid state and poured directly onto the other skin in the necessary spaces and flotation compartments. When the foam is thoroughly cured, it is sealed with cloth and resin to make the chamber watertight. Premolded and cut urethane blocks also are sealed between laminates to serve the same flotation function.

Most fiberglass yachts are made of two or more separate moldings, which are then fastened together. An exception is small dinghies and runabouts, which are cast in one piece. A hull section molding plus a deck-and-trunk cabin molding, for example, would probably comprise the typical 30-foot sailboat. These modules are then fastened together in various ways. Some kind of mechanical fastener combined with a resin bonder is most commonly employed. When two pieces of a fiberglass boat are put together, the joints are classified "primary" or "secondary." If the resin was wet when the union was made, they are primary-bonded. If the resin had cured and the two sections were joined and fastened afterward, they are deemed to be secondary-bonded.

All things being equal, the stronger of these is the primary bond as the joint is part of the structure. A well-designed boat will be conceived, and production will be planned, so that the maximum number of primary bondings may be made in construction. If the joints are well designed so that there is sufficient bearing surface and thickness to accommodate mechanical fastenings, secondary joints can be entirely satisfactory. In order to provide alignment and compression while joints are curing, as well as to fasten the components, mechanical fastenings such as through-bolts or screws are often used. Screws with prepared prethreaded holes or self-tapping screws are the least desirable fasteners in this type of construction as they have poor holding power. The through-bolt constitutes a much better fastener in this service.

The very best construction consists of the following: sections like, for example, one requiring deck-to-sheer attachment are fastened to a primary bond with Monel or stainless through-bolts. Next the edges so formed are sealed and backed up by additional tape reinforcing laminates. The joint between deck and trunk cabin has always been—both in traditional wood construction and in fiberglass—a troublesome source of leaks. For this reason many manufacturers now make trunk-cabin and deck out of one single premolded piece. Annoying joints are eliminated once and for all with this design.

The next phase of construction after the hull components are joined is to build the interior, install the engine, step the masts, if needed, and to fit the rigging. Because of the convenience in mass-production techniques and the facility with which it may be maintained by owners, builders are increasingly turning to a pre-molded fiberglass interior. Bulkheads, bunk supports, galley, even toilets and showers will be FRP. This is a welcome trend. Anything that lessens maintenance means more sailing time. In the finest construction, hardware fittings for internal molded furniture such as door locks, latches, hinges, galley pumps, will have extra plies of laminate or wood blocks to accept screw threads and backup through-bolts in order that fasteners do not pull out.

OTHER FRP CONSTRUCTION

Several other fiberglass construction methods besides hand lay-up are commonly found. The first of these is utilized in production-run manufacturing of small boats like dinghies and runabouts. Companies able to build and sell small boats in quantity are the only ones using these methods since a large capital outlay for tooling is required. Since these small utility craft form the majority of the boats in use today, a discussion of manufacturing techniques may prove useful.

Die Molding: Used for large production runs. Male-to-female molds are heated with steam or electricity. Glass cloth and resin are laid in the mold, the sections of which are clamped together by air or hydraulic pressure. When the insert has cured, the dies are opened and the piece removed.

Vacuum-Bag Molding: Fiberglass reinforcing and resin are charged into the female mold. A rubber or synthetic sheet is laid in the mold and a vacuum pump exhausts the air between the sheet, forcing it to conform to the mold. Conformance to design and glass-resin density are good with this method.

Pressure-Bag Molding: The same as the foregoing, except that instead of a vacuum, a pressure bag like a balloon is pumped up to apply pressure to the mold contents.

Flexible bag and matched die production of fiberglass boats have both advantages and disadvantages. With these techniques bubbles are reduced to a minimum and good glass density is attained. Curing of the laminate throughout takes place since glass and resin are charged into the mold at the same moment. A homogenous primary bond results with a consequent hard, uniform hull. Conscientious quality control becomes important with these techniques because fabrication success depends on proper charging of the molds by workers. Materials must be laid in the press carefully with just the proper amount of resin distributed throughout the mold before the halves are closed and pressurized. Resin richness or resin starvation can cause a faulty hull if quality control is neglected. Delamination and bubbling were common in the early days of pressurized fabrication but are rarely experienced today.

Chopped-Fiber/Resin-Gun Construction
A technique that was thought to have great promise utilized an airgun that could blow chopped strands of fiberglass onto a prepared mold and simultaneously spray a catalyzed resin onto the glass. This method eliminated hand draping of fiberglass. The gun process speeded up production of small boats and lowered manufacturing costs, so that the savings, theoretically at least, were passed on to the buyer. Quality of gun-process moldings is extremely dependent on operator skill to keep the gun moving in a manner that will ensure uniform deposit of glass strands and resin.

Recently several new methods of construction in fiberglass have appeared. None of these represents a new "system," but merely changes the nature of the reinforcing material.

Sea-Flex

A relatively new material which has appeared on the scene is sea-flex, a structural foundation material which is used in conjunction with fiberglass and resin to form hull, bulkheads, and other boat sections.

The material consists of something resembling many tubular sections of fiberglass—like round fiberglass "fishing-rods" which are lightly bonded to a flexible section of cloth. In use, the sections of sea-flex are bent around molds set on station lines and covered with glass cloth and resin coated to set. The sections can be cut with a saw to the proper shapes much like conventional planking and bulkheads, thereby eliminating the task of draping woven cloth. Sea-flex has good impact and stress resistance, and greater buoyancy than conventional fiberglass.

Graphite Fibers

The use of graphite-fiber reinforcement has just recently appeared in the marine field. The technology is a spin-off from the aerospace industry, where extremely strong yet lightweight reinforcing is vitally necessary. In the past the high cost of the material prohibited its use in boats, but recent advances in manufacturing technique and wider use has lowered the cost considerably.

Graphite is extruded in microscopic filaments or threads which are then bonded together with a sizing into a "tow." The tow is in essence a flat ribbon composed of many thousands of fibers. When wetted out with epoxy resin, the material develops extreme strength along the direction of the fibers. Graphite is superior for mast reinforcing, reinforcement of centerboards and rudders, and sections of hull where great strength without a proportional increase in weight or mass is desired. The strength increase in comparison to other materials is considerable, as Table 2 shows.

Table 2
Graphite Composite[a] Densities and Specific Moduli
Compared with Other Materials

Material	Specific Gravity	Specific Modulus (Msi)[b]
Graphite fiber[b]	1.52	11.2
Glass fiber (60%)—epoxy	1.84	3.1
Aluminum	2.78	3.6
Steel	7.85	3.7

[a]60% fiber volume in epoxy.
[b]Specific modulus = (modulus of elasticity) / (specific gravity).

Application of Graphite. Graphite tow comes on large reels with a paper interleaving. To apply, the surface to be reinforced is wetted out with epoxy resin, after which the tow is peeled from the reel and laid in wet resin. Lamination is possible by waiting until the prior layer has cured. It is in the nature of graphite construction that total hulls of the material, except in very small or dinghy sizes, is not financially feasible. On the other hand, for partial use in areas of extreme stress it is highly useful. Not the least of graphite fiber's advantages is the ease with which it lends itself to amateur building.

More information on graphite fiber construction is available from Gougeon Brothers, Inc., 706 Martin St., Bay City, MI 48706.

Kevlar

Kevlar is a new synthetic fabric which is used in somewhat the same way—that is, for reinforcing—as graphite, but it is also used as a substitute for fiberglass reinforcing cloth. Its use is not widespread enough at the present time to warrant further discussion here.

Composite Construction

A sheathing of fiberglass applied over a wood foundation will frequently be found in the construction of larger boats. Fiberglass over plywood in hard-chine design is one example of composite construction. Strip planking bent around molds or thin layers of wood veneer glued and stapled as in ashcroft planking and then covered with fiberglass are two other examples of composite construction. Sometimes the foundation may be an old wooden boat which has historic design or qualities of beauty that warrant rebuilding and restoration.

Among marine industry experts there has been some speculation vis-à-vis the advisability of combining wood and fiberglass. One view holds that each material has a different ratio of contraction and expansion when wet, and since there is a difference in the modulus of elasticity a mechanical failure of the bond is likely to occur.

Experimentation seems to indicate that this is true only for poor or difficult applications. If a thin layer of glass is applied as a "cure-all" over an oil-soaked, badly fastened, rotting hull, failure is certain. There will be working of the unsound hull and the sheathing will rupture. Water enters between the glass and the wood, the wood becomes swollen, and the fiberglass peels off. Boundary-layer water and the boat's motion finish the job by prying off the loosened sheets.

On the other hand satisfactory and even superior boats have been built with the composite method. Thickness and quality control when applying the glass and structural soundness of the foundation hull seem to be crucial.

As a general rule, fiberglass prepared according to the manufacturer's recommended procedures when applied to new wood works fine. The advantages of such application are that the wood is protected from destruction by marine organisms, water absorption is lessened (which usually makes up for the added weight of the covering), and the structural strength of the hull is greatly increased. As stated, when new wood is glassed, mechanical bonding is generally good and delamination seldom occurs.

Evidence seems to contradict the belief that covering one or both sides of wood planking causes or accelerates rot. Laboratory testing and practical experience indicate, on the contrary, that chemical constituents of the resins inhibit the growth of rot fungi.

Provided the sheathing is sufficiently thick and that good techniques are followed, old hulls can be restored and given a new lease on life with FRP sheathing.

5. Keeping Up the Fiberglass Boat

In general, maintaining the fiberglass boat requires significantly less labor than boats built with other materials. This is because the finish—the gel coat—is an integral part of the hull lamination and contains the pigment in suspension. The protective "paint" is therefore an integral part of the structure.

When a fiberglass boat is built, this first, pigmented resin coat is sprayed into the female mold. A smooth other finish is necessary to cover the warp and woof of the rough fiberglass cloth. In order to function well, the gel coat is formulated of resin having abrasion resistance, enough elasticity to "give and take" in use, and enough "memory" to be able to return to shape after flexion from impact or torsion as in sailing or bouncing against a dock. In addition, the formulation must be chemically able to hold pigment and additives to filter the sun's rays and resist deterioration owing to acids and chemicals in polluted waters.

As any boat owner knows, pleasure boats receive hard usage and the protective qualities of the gel coat are demanding. Despite the common misconception, fiberglass is not completely unporous. Gel coat must also function as a barrier to keep moisture from reaching the laminates. It helps to consider the hull as a foundation material with an outer protectant, much as one thinks of the "paint" on a steel, aluminum, or wood boat. In this view, owners of fiberglass craft should perhaps expend more care on this vital outer layer.

EXTERIOR

Generally speaking, procedures to keep up a fiberglass boat surface are quite similar to maintaining an automobile finish. A clean, glossy surface with some hard protective film as a sealant coat is the desired objective.

In Chapter 3 procedures for cleaning are discussed, but it will be beneficial to elaborate further here. In addition to thorough cleaning on a weekly and monthly basis, plus fitting-out and decommissioning cleanings, the boat should be given a once-over each evening during the season. Use a big sponge, a soft scrubbing brush, or a long-handled sponge mop with a mild household detergent to remove salt and dust, and then hose down with fresh water. This will help maintain the "showroom shine" indefinitely.

STAIN REMOVAL

Solvents like gasoline, benzine, or kerosene may be used to remove grease, oil, or tar stains. Care should be taken using an automotive tar remover on boat surfaces because some of them will cause failure or wrinkling of the gel coat. Try a small inconspicuous part of the hull before you swab it on. No solvent of any kind should be left

for any time on the gel coat. Keep a bucket of warm sudsy
water and a hose handy to wash and rinse the surface as
soon as the stain disappears.

Detergent washings are sometimes not strong enough
to remove stains left by some organic substances which
have penetrated into gel coat. A common household
cleanser with a chlorine bleach will often remove coffee
or food stains. Do not overscrub. Work lightly a little at
a time, allowing the bleach a chance to break down the
stain without a lot of abrasion.

One of the most troublesome stains on fiberglass is
rust. Such stains can appear within hours and are difficult
to remove. A tool or tin can left in the overnight dew can
result in an ugly iron-oxide stain the next day. The best
thing to do is to avoid leaving things on deck in the first
place. But once rust stains appear, stain removers which
do not harm fiberglass are available at marine suppliers.
It would be advisable to test these first to be sure there
is no deleterious effect on your finish.

Oxalic acid in a weak solution will remove rust, but the
solution must be made up quite dilute and should be
flushed off with water as soon as the stain is eradicated.
If left too long, the gel coat will soften. Therefore, apply
it only long enough to bleach lightly and then flush the
surface quickly. Many short-term applications will prove
more satisfactory than a single long-term one. Observe
precautions printed on the box to prevent skin burns
from handling the acid.

If local stain removal plus cleaning is not sufficient to
bring the hull up to standard, then you should try one of
the special-formula liquid cleaner/polishes (see the list
of suppliers at the end of Chapter 3). Most of these
concoctions are in liquid form and contain a preparation
which cleans and also leaves a thin, waxy protective film.
Buffing with a soft rag or a lambswool pad after application sets the sheen. Again, be sure to follow the printed

directions. When buffed, evaluate the surface to decide whether you will finish with a hard wax or if still further measures are needed. If the surface is dull or chalked, then you will have to try a rubbing compound.

The pigmentation of gel coat has a tendency to fade because of weathering from the ozone and ultraviolet rays of the sun. A mild abrasive such as is formulated in any number of "fiberglass paste cleaners" will cut a microscopically thin layer of gel coat to slough off dead pigment. This will leave sound, bright pigment. Preparations of this kind are sold by most marine suppliers under the brand names of many different manufacturers (see the list at the end of Chapter 3).

Paste cleaners are mild rubbing compounds which are poured on wet, folded cheesecloth and rubbed in a circular motion much as with auto rubbing compounds; this will remove the old dead layer. It is followed by a washing to remove grit. Next, a polishing with one of the carnauba waxes should be undertaken. If the paste cleaner is not strong enough, your next alternative is to try one of the milder auto rubbing compounds, but be sure to try it first on a less visible part of the hull where failure will not show.

If a more spartan approach is called for, you can sand with #800-grit wet-or-dry sandpaper. It is a drastic measure and can work only once, for too much gel coat is removed at each sanding. After one sanding the hull will probably have to be painted the following year unless it is kept up exceptionally well. If any of the above maintenance tricks work, be sure to keep what you have gained by continual care.

A word about applying wax. Do not work on large areas at a single time. Instead, divide the surface into small patches. The boat should also be out of the sun where the wax will not dry too quickly to make polishing difficult. When buffing wax, you can use a pad or lambswool disc on a drill or buffer, but be sure to keep the drill or buffer moving so that you do not cut through the gel coat. Be especially careful when buffing corners or edges, as the pad can quickly cut through if pressure is applied. The rule is keep the buffer moving and do not push!

When you buy wax for fiberglass, try to get one especially made for boats. These formulations have been put together by manufacturers whose chemical labs understand the difference between the resins of epoxy and polyester as found in boat gel coat as opposed to the lacquer finishes of autos. Fiberglass wax is also loaded with fillers to block the voids in gel coat surface pores. Ultraviolet-filter additives to retard color fading, and vehicles for easy applications in the adverse conditions found in most boatyards, are also mixed into boat FRP wax.

You can ease the labor of heavy-duty waxings by using a light-duty clean-and-wax spray during the season in areas that receive extra wear. Decks, cabin tops, cockpits, and areas subjected to sun and wear can be sprayed directly as required. This lays down a thin layer of protective film and prevents accumulation of superficial dirt.

When buffing gel coat, always be careful that you do not remove too much material. For this reason hand buffing, despite the work, is preferred over machine buffing. One test for safe polishing is to look at the rag or pad after some rubbing. If the color is a light shade of the gel coat color, the buffing is proper; if it is a deep, dark shade, then too much gel coat is being removed and a mottled surface will result. Less damage is done to gel coat when it is regularly used and cleaned during the season than during storage, so it is a good idea to wash and wax just before storage to provide a protective coating during the long winter months.

Painting the Fiberglass Hull

When hard usage, repairs and patches to the hull, or deterioration of the gel coat make restoring a boat's finish impossible, it will be necessary to paint. No definitive statement can be made as to how long the original finish applied by the manufacturer will last in normal service. Six years, depending on the thickness, pigment loading, color, and quality of the gel coat, should be the minimum. I have seen fiberglass boats over twenty years old that have been routinely well cared for and the finish is still as fine as when first built.

If chalking is the only sign of deterioration and the pigment is still alive and uniform, repainting is not necessary—the polishing and rubbing techniques will work well. Fading, which is extensive with certain colors like dark red or blue, is caused by the sun's rays and is greatest in southern waters. Sometimes buffing and polishing will work, but generally repainting is required. It is in the nature of certain colors that they will go down more quickly than others. The consequent increased demand for maintenance means that a minute amount of pigment is removed with each polishing and the white undercoat of the laminate will show through. Black is especially prone to this phenomenon.

Be Careful of Color

Lighter colors are, generally speaking, more resistant to chalking and fading than darker colors. On the other hand the beauty of fine, glossy blacks, blues, reds, and greens is an appealing motive for their use. From a subjective point of view it might be safe to say that your favorite colors will remain pleasant over the long haul. Many unusual colors—chartreuse, purples, yellows, and wild pastels—will become unpleasing after the first enthusiasm has worn off and are also alien to the traditions of the sea.

Cabin and Interior
White is beautiful, functional, and traditional. It is not the case that "white shows the dirt," as folklorically believed. In reality it is easier to keep up white with cleaning and touch-up than the darker colors. Because interiors tend to be cramped, the cheerful, light, airy colors are to be preferred. Varnish is indeed beautiful, but works best on vessels with large ports and windows which pass sufficient light below. What looks quite good is a lighter tint of the deck color set off with varnish or contrasting trim. Cream, off-white, or ivory is a good choice, and the sameness can be relieved with colorful curtains, bunk covers, and pillows.

CHOICE OF PAINT

Choice of a paint system for your boat will be determined by the use to which it will be put. The concept of surface coatings as a "system" complete in itself has been discussed in Chapter 2, as have the characteristics of the different paints. Now would be a good time to review that chapter before picking a paint. If the hull is troublesome, an epoxy-base paint will probably be preferable as the bonding tenacity of epoxy is high. It is true that chalking is more prevalent with epoxies, but this must be balanced out against their bonding advantages over other formulations. Epoxies are generally sold as two-part mixtures, and present no problem if the instructions on the can are followed.

With polyurethane a tough, color-retentive and chalking-resistant coating results. These paints are usually available already blended. Acrylic and alkyd paints are also available, but I do not think they should be used on hull or topsides exterior as they tend to be too soft. They work well, however, on interior joinerwork. The epoxies and polyurethanes have, in my opinion, more to recommend them for plastic hulls.

When you have decided on a paint, stick to the "system" written in the manufacturer's literature or on the can. Use only solvents and thinners that are recommended, and do not mix brands or take shortcuts. Not all solvents are compatible with all paints, and failure can occur if you try to beat the "system."

Topsides

You can't go wrong with white for topsides. It is traditional, pleasant, and clean looking. Although tire fender marks show more on white, it is actually more easily touched up and kept clean looking than some of the dark colors. White will make a boat look larger, whereas the dark colors tend to make a boat look smaller. White can also be used to create the illusion of lowness in a high, boxy hull.

Decks

There are several factors to be considered in choosing deck color. Light decks will reflect the sun and keep things cooler underfoot and below. If you operate in southern waters this might be good to remember. Deck color should also be chosen to harmonize with the overall color scheme. Also, deck color can be used to "point up" the best lines of your boat. The darker colors tend to absorb the sun's rays and heat up things down below. This is useful operating in northern latitudes. It is often useful to tint the deck colors slightly on deckhouses and in front of the steering stations in order that a species of "snow blindness" not occur. It is well to remember that

dark decks painted over light topsides colors tend to
make a boat look top-heavy.

Superstructure
The superstructure is generally painted the same color
as the topsides. Lighter shades of the topside color can
be utilized to make a trunk cabin, raised deck, or dog-
house look lower.

Below the Waterline
On the bottom, the antifouling properties are more important than the color. On sailboats, however, a good
portion of the bottom is exposed when the ship heels and
this must be taken into account. Good boottop lining
between the topside and bottom can accentuate the
flowing lines of good design.

ORGANIZING AND PLANNING THE WORK

If your choice is to repaint the boat, the job of organizing
the work is important to successful application. Obvious
as it is, get the boat hauled. Don't attempt to paint topsides while the boat is in the water. I have seen such jobs
and they are never satisfactory. Only minor touch-up
should be attempted afloat. Repainting absolutely de-
mands the controlled conditions of working ashore.

Before beginning work, make an effort to place the
boat in an area that is shaded from direct sunlight so that
accelerated drying will not cause laps to show. In the
better professional boatyards, a building is utilized for a
paint shed because environment is considered a major
factor in obtaining a good paint job. It is often possible
to stretch plastic tarpaulins and staple them over temporary supports to shield the work from the sun. Since
airborne dust is the greatest enemy of a good paint job,

the tarps will also serve to keep down dust. It is a good idea to wet down the area with a hose before painting begins.

The boat should be well shored so that there is no strain or stress on the hull, but at the same time the shoring should be planned so that the poppets may easily be moved one at a time when it becomes time to paint the underbody. Be sure the hull can be reached easily for working. Do not rely on a ladder, but obtain sawhorses and erect a scaffolding clear along each side of the boat. Once painting starts it is a nuisance to have to stop to move the working platform. Occasionally more than one person will be working at a time and a proper scaffolding will simplify this.

SEQUENCE

Putting the paint on usually goes pretty quickly. It is in the planning, the collection of necessary supplies and tools, and in surface preparation that most time is lost.

It is my opinion that the best plan is to start on all underwater ironwork like iron ballast keels and steel centerboards first. The logic for this lies in the fact that the only thing that keeps ironwork from deteriorating due to galvanic corrosion is the paint barrier. Therefore, the more and thicker the paint coats you are able to apply before launching, the better. Because it is preferable to have thorough drying between successive coats of Rustoleum, zinc chromate, or red lead—whatever you use for a primer—it is useful to begin here and put on a fresh coat as each one dries. In the interim you can be working on another part of the boat.

A technique which I have now tried and can heartily recommend on this problem of ballast keels and steel centerboards is to go to bare metal and then epoxy the metal. It is advantageous to borrow or rent a large, heavy-duty disc sander and to purchase coarse emery discs. Take the ironwork down until it is bright with, at the most, only rust pits showing. Wipe it with a solvent like acetone and then paint with several thick coatings of catalyzed epoxy resin. After the resin dries a coat or two of the regular bottom paint is applied. If the job is properly done and there are no voids for the water to enter, rusted ironwork ceases to be a major problem.

A sailboat should next have her masts and booms painted so that drips to the deck can be removed. If the spars are aluminum, a film oxidation preventive like Sparcote can be applied and drips wiped up. Masts for raising and lowering the dinghy, antenna supports, and flag masts in power boats should now be done.

Because it is invariably necessary to tread on the trunk cabin top and deck in the course of the work, I like to go to the topsides next and leave the decks till last so they are pristine when the boat is launched. I do the bottom the very last because bottom paint has a tendency to be runny and messy, and while it is possible to cut in bottom paint over topside, the reverse is impossible.

It doesn't make much difference when the interior is painted, but it should be completed and well dried before there is a lot of traffic in and out during subsequent work.

PREPARATION OF THE SURFACE

The most important factor in attaining a quality paint job is how well you prepare the surface. Time spent on this phase will pay off later. Slap-dash or scrimped shortcuts are bound to appear in peeling paint or bleeding topsides before many weeks go by. Proper preparation will prevent failure and guarantee a good mechanical and chemical bond. If you go slow now it will go faster later.

Topsides and Superstructure

A thorough cleaning begins surface preparation; give the ship a good scrubbing with hot water and detergent, and then rinse the soap and dirt off with the hose. Now, closely inspect surfaces and note down scratches and gouges that must be filled. This is the best time to evaluate the structural strength of the skin layer. Make a close search for fracture lines in the skin that may indicate stress due to flexing of the fiberglass. If there are any indications of flexion fracture, Chapter 6 will outline procedures for repair and reinforcement to correct the problem.

Removing the waxy mold-release agent used by manufacturers and residual wax and polish is the next step. Neglecting to remove this film, it has been my experience, is the primary cause of paint failure in the "system process." No paint can bond well chemically with a slippery, incompatible barrier between it and the foundation material.

Begin to amass a pile of clean rags and purchase a generous supply of solvent. Methyl-ethylketone, toluol, and acetone are the usual solvents for this purpose. Some marine paint companies sell a specially formulated wax/mold-release-agent solvent at a slightly more expensive price. Either dewaxers or raw solvents will work equally well.

The hull should now be divided mentally into small areas or segments, fourths for a small boat or sixths or eights with a larger boat. Choose a portlight or fitting of some kind as the limit of a particular area. This is important so that you remember where you left off and no portion of the topsides is inadvertently skipped. It is not sufficient to dampen a rag and wipe for this will just spread the dissolved chemicals and wax around from one place to another. The proper procedure is to really saturate the rag and wipe in a downward stroke toward the waterline, resoaking the rag as the solvent dries or is used up. Discard the rag frequently and take a fresh one as the old one is impregnated with the removed wax.

When the whole hull including trunk cabin and deck —if you are repainting these—is finished, again scrub the boat with warm water and detergent or Spic and Span to remove residue dissolved by the solvent and any film left by the solvent itself.

Next you should sand the whole hull, using a medium-grade production paper like #80. Every inch of the hull will be covered with this hand sanding so gouges and scrapes that must be filled will be evident. When sanding is finished, wipe off the sanding dust with a solvent-dampened rag and again wash with detergent and warm water and hose down.

Now fillers, fiberglass putties, or glazing compounds— many different names are utilized—will be employed to fill niches and build up indentations level with the original surface. There are two basic kinds of filler available: one has an epoxy base, the other a polyester-styrene base. Either works well on polyester laminate boats, which are the majority. I believe that the epoxy fillers give a better bond with old surface. To bulk out these compounds, several different kinds of fillers are used. Milled fibers, chopped fiberglass strands, or colloidal silica powder are some. Many epoxy putties formulated for use in auto body shops use metallic particles for bulk, and these auto types should never be used in boat work as rusting and bleeding-through may occur. Fiberglassing surfacing putties come with the catalyst mixed in and also with a catalyst that must be added by the user.

For proper application the compound should be the consistency of soft butter. It should be deposited on a piece of clean glass or smooth plywood used as a palette. Only the tip of a very flexible putty knife should pick up a small quantity of filler and then carry it to the indentation to be filled. The blade should be wide enough to overlap the gouge or hole generously. For deep holes, several thin passes—allowing each layer to set up a little before application of the next layer—works best. This technique makes for less shrinkage and a better bond. The final pass should leave filler a little higher than the surrounding surface as some shrinking will occur and some excess material is desirable for sanding flush. After "glazing," filled areas should be sanded by hand with a #320 production paper and finished off with a #600 wet-or-dry sanded wet.

Bottoms

With a few exceptions the bottom is prepared exactly like the topsides. If your bottom paint is a metallic formulation like copper-bottom or mercury paint, it will slough off liberally during the scrubbing. A stiff, brown-bristled, long-handled brush should be used in this operation, and care should be taken that nothing splashes in the eyes as these are extremely caustic paints. It is strongly recommended that goggles be worn when sanding, washing, and painting bottoms with antifouling preparations. Especially dangerous to the eyes are powerdriven wire brushes. This is because off-abraded material and small pieces of broken wire bristles fly about with great force. A respirator or gauze mask should be worn when sanding beneath the hull because copper, mercury, TBTO, and TBTF paints are extremely toxic and can cause damage to the lungs. Better yet, a respirator should be worn during *any* sanding whatsoever.

Use of Paint Removers

Synthetic fiberglass topside paints are thin, hard formulations and rarely will a paint remover be necessary to take off built-up coats. On the other hand, bottom paints, because they are thick with metallic pigments, build up much more quickly. Sometimes, therefore, a paint remover will be necessary. A better procedure is to remove the excess coats with a power sander, but if this is too slow, a chemical remover is feasible.

Chemical paint removers are very powerful concentrations and should be handled according to the recommendations printed on the label. Test an inconspicuous portion of the bottom to be sure the gel coat is not damaged by the remover. Dab on the remover, letting it remain only long enough for the old paint to wrinkle and lift. Scrape off the lifted paint with a sharp putty knife and immediately neutralize the patch by wiping with a solvent-soaked rag. Never leave remover on longer than necessary to lift the old paint. When all the old antifouling has been removed, wash the bottom with warm water and detergent and hose off to rinse and neutralize the remover.

On Priming Systems

It is always good practice not to pile on more coats of paint than necessary to protect the boat and maintain good looks. But what about priming?

Most manufacturers of paint designed for use with fiberglass also make a foundation primer. Many recommend that a priming coat of their own brand be applied as a first step in preparation of the surface. In general, however, I would say that with the exception of new work, only in cases where a paint is formulated so that a priming coat *must* be used as part of the system for proper chemical bonding, priming is rarely necessary if the foundation coat is in good condition—that is, when it is of compatible formulation (read the can!) and has good mechanical bond to the glass of the hull.

If, however, the old coat is in bad shape, glazing and sanding to a smooth surface and priming is to be heartily recommended. A "nonsanding" primer has been formulated by one paint company. The primer prepares the surface for receiving the final coat by making the surface "tacky" to provide good chemical bond. This product functions as a chemical pretreatment for use with the manufacturer's own paints. Controlled drying time is essential with the primer, and it cannot be permitted to dry for more than two or three hours or adhesion to the final coat suffers. It is my opinion that sanding smooths, fairs, and etches the surface for paint adhesion in a superior manner, and that the habitual use of "nonsanding" primers is to be discouraged.

Describing surface preparation in words is a simple thing, but the process is something else. All work must be done conscientiously and no corners should be cut. When you are satisfied with the condition of the boat, painting can begin.

PAINTING

When preparation is complete, painting should proceed immediately. A quiet, windless day should be picked, and if the boat is in the direct rays of the sun, some shading arrangement must be rigged so the hull is in shadow. If paints are applied in the sun, laps dry so quickly that they cannot be worked out and are highly visible.

Strict attention must be given to the manufacturer's instructions on the label of the can. This is especially necessary if you are using the one- or two-part epoxy or other plastic-base paints, because mixing and thinning of these paints is highly critical.

For brushing on paint, the term "flowability" has been coined to describe the self-leveling ability which permits the paint to spread and eliminate brushmarks. This quality is maximum at the consistency that the paint comes from the can. In general, the volatiles in paint as it comes from the can evaporate and the mixture thickens. In this condition, and sometimes even right from the can, the paint is stiff and doesn't brush out well. To overcome this many professional boat painters will thin paint just a little; it makes the paint easier to work. Some small amount of coverability is lost, but this is worth it in ease of working. Some deftness with the brush will keep bristle marks to a minimum and help the paint to "hide." Even though thinned once, the volatiles will evaporate while you are working and the paint will become stiff again. Professionals, therefore, add minute quantities, on the order of tablespoonsful, whenever they notice the paint becoming stiff. Do not add more than tiny amounts or the paint will become too thin to hide. Be sure to stir the paint while working as thinners tend to rise to the top.

Loading the Brush
The quality of the final job will benefit if the brush is kept clean and drip-free. A brush should be dipped into the paint only one-third to one-half the bristle length. Excess should be removed by gently tapping the bristles inside the can. Do not get rid of excess paint by scraping the edge of the brush across the lip of the can. This destroys the natural shaping of the bristles. The paint you are using to dip your brush in will have been drawn off the original can into a clean can holding only about 3 or 4 inches. Before pouring paint from the manufacturer's can, take a nail or an icepick and punch holes at 2-inch intervals around the lip of the can to keep it clean by permitting slopped paint to drain back into the can.

Most expert yacht painters make strokes in every direction to work the paint into the pores and then finish off with all the strokes going in the same direction. The brush should glide easily and barely touch against the surface being painted. If the brush drags, it is not loaded with sufficient paint or the paint is too thick. Do not scrub. Lay the paint on ahead of the last place you painted which is still wet and work backward toward the wet patch while blending in the laps with light strokes. Do not attempt to remove insects or leaves which might blow upon the fresh paint. When the paint dries you can just brush with a clean cloth and the marks left will be barely visible.

Painting the Bottom

Fiberglass is largely immune to the destructive effects of marine borers and this is one of its great advantages over wood. Many a wooden ship has been sent to the bottom by the teredo, the gribble, and the Spaeroma, or "putty bug." Fortunately, none of these fellows cares to chew fiberglass; but this does not mean that you can get away without antifouling. Marine algaes, bryozoans like tube-worms, as well as barnacles, attach themselves to fiber-glass quite happily. Once attached, they grow into large colonies that accumulate shells and disfigure the hull streamlining to such an extent that fuel consumption, speed, and performance under sail are adversely affected.

The traditional method to prevent this is to protect the surface with a poison suspended in the bottom paint. This toxin slowly exfoliates or leaches its poison into the water environment, killing or discouraging the free-swimming larvae of these organisms. The thin paint film on the bottom is the vehicle that carries the suspended toxin; how well that film serves to repel fouling is a function of how well the paint sticks to the hull.

Many different compounds work as antifouling. The

older ones contain a metallic toxicant such as copper or mercury. For some twenty years now we have also seen paints containing an organo-tin antifoulant such as tri-butyl-tin fluoride (TBTF).

At this writing these new organo-tin paints have received a good reception and work quite well. Though originally developed for aluminum and steel to avoid galvanic corrosion from the dissimilar metals, TBTO and TBTF are now also added to most metallic paints and are suitable for fiberglass boats. The organo-tin antifouling paints are fine for boats that are habitually trailered or stored ashore between launching and use. (See the discussion of paints in Chapter 2.)

There are two types of antifoulants suitable for fiberglass—semisoft or hard. The semisoft turn porous and allow the toxicants to work gradually toward the surface at a controlled rate. The binder of the hard antifoulants holds much more tenaciously than the binder of the soft ones.

Vinyl-base antifouling paints are now widely in use, but like lacquer, vinyl needs a harsh solvent to keep pigment in suspension and there is a risk that it will lift off old nonvinyl paint that may be on the hull. Vinyl-on-vinyl will usually be compatible, but if there is any doubt, try a test patch in an inconspicuous place. If the paint does not wrinkle or lift off, the formulas will work together. The vehicle of vinyl paint is very long-lasting, and sometimes paint will look good to the eye after a season's use. Don't be tempted to go another season, because the binder may look good but the toxins will have become exhausted and the antifouling effect will certainly be marginal. Make it a practice to renew bottom paint in accordance with custom in your port or in line with the manufacturer's recommendations.

If there is heavy fouling in your boating area, it may be worthwhile to put on two coats of antifouling. This more than doubles the protection. Don't sand between coats; rely instead on good brushwork to keep the bottom smooth. It is preferable to use a wide brush to get the job over with as soon as possible and not spend more time than necessary under the hull. The toxins in the paint are metallic flakes which will sink to the bottom of the can; stir the paint constantly so they do not sink and thin out the mixture.

If radio ground plates or sacrificial zincs are painted over they will be ineffective, so be careful not to do so. Be sure the barrier coating is dried and thick before applying cuprous oxide paints to iron and steel underwater fittings or there will be galvanic corrosion. Intake screens must not be painted heavily enough to block the passage holes or slits which allow cooling water to enter; at the same time, through-hull fittings, intakes and outlets for sinks, engine cooling, and pump discharges are a favorite place for barnacles and algae to collect. Two barnacles can plug a drain or lower cooling water efficiency sufficiently to overheat an engine dangerously. Wrap a cloth around a dowel stick and get some antifouling into these fittings.

Never thin antifouling paint. Just the opposite of topsides paint—the thicker it goes on, the better. Do not go clear to the boottop when painting but stop about ½ inch short. After the bottom is finished, go back with a flexible, large, well-shaped brush and cut in the bottom to the waterline. If the boottop lines are well scribed, this is facilitated. It would be useful if manufacturers of fiberglass boats molded in these lines because scribing destroys the surface of the gel coat at the waterline. Masking tape can be used to keep a straight line, though it is the devil itself to get on straight. Be sure to pull off the tape before the paint has set, and press it down well before painting.

Remember, if surface preparation has been done as recommended here, and if you read the manufacturer's instructions, a workmanlike fiberglass paint job will inevitably result.

6. Common Repairs and Modifications to the Fiberglass Boat: How to Make Them

The technology of working with fiberglass is in a constant state of development and change. It is difficult to make any definitive statements about formulations or working techniques without running the risk of being behind the times. Nonetheless, there are certain broad general statements that can be made which will be helpful. One of these is that a repair with fiberglass and resin is necessary if your boat is to be properly maintained. It will pay to learn how to make simple surface repairs, patch punctures, and fabricate necessary joinerwork and modifications.

The boats you will have to deal with will be laid up primarily in polyester resin. To make repairs you can choose between polyester or epoxy resin techniques. Polyester resin is the same as the original building material and is less costly; epoxy is more expensive but has other advantages to recommend it. Epoxy shrinks less in curing than does polyester, and it has greater mechanical and chemical bonding characteristics. More time is allowed for careful work as it usually has a longer pot life before beginning to gel. A strong and satisfactory bond is made with polyester, but pot life tends to be short and it is advisable to have some experience with smaller projects before beginning on your boat. Epoxy, in my opinion, is preferred for small surface gouges. Polyester's chemical and mechanical bonding properties are slightly less than epoxy, but nonetheless good.

Where holes, fractures, and splits are of fairly moderate size, polyester is preferable. By way of example, epoxy, because of its strong bonding qualities, would be better for filling in gel coat wrinkling and crazing or for scrapes and fractures that do not penetrate the laminates. The reason for preferring epoxy is that in non-penetrating defects there is little bonding surface or fracture depth to keep the filling material in, so the better the chemical bond of the material the more probable you will obtain a lasting repair.

For extensive holing or fractures, removal of damaged material and feathering back to good glass allows sufficient bearing surface so that adequate bond and sufficient new material can be used to warrant polyester resin. Like the problems run into by a dentist, minor cavities are sometimes harder to fix permanently than larger ones which can be drilled out to hold the filling. A good idea is to use epoxy for minor repairs and polyester for extensive ones.

For the fiberglass-yacht owner, emergency bosun's stores should contain one or more epoxy fiberglass repair kits. These kits contain a piece of fiberglass mat, cloth, resin, and catalyst. Polyester repair kits are also made, but the shelf life of polyester is shorter and ideally the kit will never have to be used. The purpose of having a kit aboard is to make emergency patches inside or outside the hull above the waterline in case of holing caused by collision or grounding.

Kits can be bought already assembled, but tend to be

inadequate in the amount of materials supplied. It would be better to prepare your own kit, making sure that it contains resin, catalyst, promoter (to speed cure when it is necessary that the mix set up quickly), fiberglass mat, cloth, and tape. (The tape is handy for mending broken spars.) Several quarts of solvent or acetone for cleanup should be packed in a locker. The cans should be checked often for rust or leaks, as a quart of acetone will raise hell in the bilges of a fiberglass yacht if it gets loose. Varnishing the bottoms of the cans will help prevent rust, or the acetone can be stored in well-padded bottles.

WORKING WITH FIBERGLASS AND RESINS

Now is a good time for a general discussion of principles that will guarantee good results. Patching with fiberglass, if properly done, will produce a surface having a structural strength nearly equal to the original. Temperatures for proper cure should be in the neighborhood of 70° Fahrenheit; the higher the temperature, the quicker the resin will cure. Surfaces must be dry and free of oil or grease. You should try to buy components in the smallest packaging available when purchasing resin and catalyst, as deterioration is quick once the cans are open. One-quart sizes are the smallest available at the present time—which is too bad, for pint and half-pint packaging would be economical and handy for small repair jobs. If you find it necessary to make repairs in cool weather, a few infrared heat lamps in clip-on spring sockets will help to speed cure.

There is one problem inherent in working with resin: the deeper the catalyzed resin is in the container, the faster it sets up. On the other hand the resin you brush on the piece of glass used to make the patch is fairly thin in comparison. If you use a coffee can or similar deep receptacle for catalyzed resin, the stuff in the can will always set up before the coat on the patch has become tacky. Paradoxically, most manufacturers recommend that the second coat not be applied until the first has begun to set. So here we have what seems like an unsolvable problem. The way to beat this is to attack it from two angles.

First, you can lengthen the setting time of the catalyzed resin in the container you are working with. This permits smooth draping of cloth, better saturation with resin, and time for careful workmanship. The best way to do this is to use a very shallow container to hold the activated resin. I have found useful the thin, pressed-aluminum throw-away loaf pans that can be purchased in any hardware or housewares store. These permit resin to spread out to about ½ inch deep, which slows down gelling, yet they hold enough liquid to wet out a good-size patch.

The second angle is to mix only small portions of catalyzed resin at a time in a single pan. After using the contents, throw the pan away and use a fresh one for the next batch of resin.

You will now have to make an exception to the rule of following the manufacturer's recommendations explicitly and work out a small-quantity mixing formula for your own needs. This is done quite easily. Generally, in the quart size, a small bottle of catalyst is packaged with the resin. The directions usually read, "for ¼ can of resin, use ¼ bottle of catalyst; for ½, use ½; for ¾, use ¾; and for the whole quart, use the whole bottle." However, you will often want to use less than ¼ quart. When making a small patch that must be saturated several times with resin, the ¼ quart will set up in the can while you are waiting for the first coat on the patch to become tacky according to the instructions. This is frustrating and an enraging waste of resin—which is not cheap.

There is a way to beat this racket. In the beginning of the job, since it is necessary to put a foundation coat of resin on the surface being covered, and then to saturate the patch itself, a good quantity (¼ quart) of resin will be used. Mix up ¼ quart of resin per instructions, then add the catalyst as recommended. (If the catalyst container does not have graduated markings printed on the bottle or tube, take a grease pencil and make a mark at ½ the contents by eyeball estimate. Then make two more, indicating ¼ and ¾ of the contents. Now do the same thing with the can of resin.)

In adding the first ¼ of the catalyst to the resin, instead of just squirting it in count the drops till the bottle is emptied to the ¼ mark. You can do this easily by inverting the bottle or tube and squeezing gently as you would with an eye dropper. From time to time turn the catalyst tube right-side-up and check how close you are to the mark.

When the tube or bottle has been emptied right to the ¼ mark, you will have counted 20, 30, 40 drops or so. You have now created a usable measure which will allow you to find a properly curable catalyst-to-resin ratio for any amount of resin you will need. Next you can mix up a small trial quantity of resin to cover a tool box, for example, and keep track of the amount of resin and the number of drops you mixed in. The gel time of this trial batch will determine the ratio of catalyst to resin for future batches. As long as the manufacturer's catalyst or one very similar is used, and a strict count of the number of drops is kept, this technique will work with any brand of resin. Now if you need only ⅛ of the quart of resin, just use half the number of drops you used for the first ¼, and so forth.

When a practical catalyst-to-resin ratio is established with this procedure, not only will you be able to mix nonstandard amounts for special jobs, but more important, you will have a method for varying the curing time of a mix. If your first attempt sets up too quickly or more slowly than you wish, a few drops more or less will shift the gel time in the direction you want.

It pays to be sure that you mix catalyst thoroughly to achieve a uniform rate of cure. If you use an aluminum throw-away loaf pan when adding catalyst, tilt the pan so that the liquid is all in one end where it can be well stirred. When you vary catalyst quantities it is probable that you will increase rather than decrease the amount over the manufacturer's instructions. This means that the resin and catalyst will not come out even and you will end up short of catalyst, so be sure to buy an extra tube of catalyst when you obtain the resin. The pot life of catalyzed resin can be further lengthened by avoiding direct sunlight and by keeping the container in a flat pan of ice water to slow down gel time.

BE AWARE OF SAFETY

Curing of polyester resin is a thermal reaction as catalyzation releases heat and raises the resin temperature. The quicker the reaction, the more heat is released. Overcatalyzation is dangerous as fire or even, under the right conditions, an explosion could result. I am not talking here about just a few drops of catalyst—it is a matter of common sense. I mean dousing resin with catalyst to attempt a near instantaneous cure. If extremely fast cures are necessary, then a promoter can be added to speed cure. Promoters are sold by the makers of the resin you choose, and work by enhancing catalyst action. To use them, add controlled amounts directly to the resin first—and mix well—then add and mix the catalyst. *Do not mix catalyst and promoter together in the absence of resin —an explosion will take place! Follow directions carefully when working with promoter.*

Do not breathe resin fumes more than is absolutely necessary. While working in the interior, forced ventilation with a fan and large-diameter flexible tubing is an excellent practice. Permit no open flames; do not smoke (preferably ever!). If the recommended procedures as delineated here are followed, there is no risk involved, which is as it should be.

On "Bargain" Glass Fabrics

In various industries today there are many applications for fiberglass cloth besides making FRP boats. Fabric of all kinds is made. To permit some fabrics to perform properly on the loom, many have the glass filaments "sized" with a lubricant. If the fabric is to be used as a reinforcing material, this sizing is dissolved off after weaving and the cloth is treated to increase tensile strength and resin absorption. This treatment is expensive and raises the cost of good reinforcing fabric. Some trade names for boating fabric are "chromed finish" and "blue sheened," for example.

Flea markets and jobbers sometimes offer cloth for cut-rate prices. This is usually untreated fabric with the sizing still in it. It will not take resin well, nor will it drape without bubbles and voids. Beware of such "bargain" cloth and be certain that the material you purchase is marine quality. You can sometimes get good prices by shopping around, but look out for super-bargain cloth.

Cautions for Glass Fabric

Small fragments of glass filaments—measuring in microns—break loose from the cloth and imbed in the skin where they are extremely irritating. Especially if you are an allergic type—and even if you are not—they can cause severe itching and discomfort. Always wear long-sleeved clothing with collars that can be buttoned up around the neck. Protective creams to prevent irritation should be applied to the face and hands.

Persons with a history of respiratory problems such as asthma or chronic colds should be careful—particles of glass cloth in the lungs do no good. A respirator should *always* be worn when sanding fiberglass; do not use a gauze or paper mask—these are not foolproof enough. Buy a properly filtered respirator.

SOME TRICKS OF THE TRADE

If you are cutting glass for patches, first fit the cloth to the surface you are repairing, mark the cloth with a felt-tip pen, and then cut it. Don't just apply resin to the area, drape the cloth, and cut off excess cloth after the resin has set. A well-tailored fit is much too difficult to achieve that way. A staple gun is handy to use when draping cloth. If you use Monel staples and they do not show, they can be left in and resined right over. Do not use common metal staples.

When stretching cloth over an edge or a difficult curve, for a better fit leave 5 or 6 inches of cloth to overlap. If only an inch or so of cloth is allowed, it is hard to get the material to lie against the surface and an air bubble will develop. On the subject of air bubbles, look for them and deal with them as you go along before the resin becomes hard; once the resin cures they are impossible to remove without sanding down and patching.

When repairing holes with fiberglass mat and cloth, the preferred method is to wet both sides of the material. Place the patch on a piece of waxed paper or cellophane, wet it with resin thoroughly, then apply it to the repair surface. Next, peel off the cellophane and wet out the outer side. This is better than the "dry" method where the repair surface is wetted, the patch placed against it and the patch outer surface wetted. Incomplete saturation, resin starvation, voids, and air bubbles are more likely with the latter method. Unless it is impossible for some reason, both sides should be resined, especially with mat or woven roving where the fabric is thick and not absorptive of resin.

Tools and Material for Repairs

- Respirator or mask
- Power saber or hand keyhole saw
- Power sander (disc type with attachment for buffing pad)
- ¼-inch electric drill
- Carbide drill burrs
- Assorted Carborundum drill tips
- Lambswool buffing pad
- Sanding block
- Scissors
- Rubber squeegee
- Putty knives
- Paintbrushes
- Clean white cloths
- Cellophane (Handi-Wrap types will do)
- Masking tape
- Single-edge razor blades
- Fiberglass rubbing compounds (coarse and medium fine)
- Fiberglass carnauba wax
- Milled fibers or patching putty
- Acetone or fiberglass washing solvents
- Cardboard
- Brown wrapping paper for masking
- Sheet aluminum for backing forms
- Soft wire
- Several short wooden sticks

- Sanding discs: #24, #60, and #100 grit
- Aluminum oxide production paper: #50, #100, and #220 grit
- Wet-or-dry sandpaper: #400 and #600 grit
- Matching gel coat
- Fiberglass mat, woven roving, and cloth
- Resin
- Catalyst

REPAIRS YOU CAN DO

Minor damage to the gel coat and/or the first laminate, and small fractures or holes which may or may not penetrate through the laminate layers, are basic repairs to fiberglass that the boat owner can profitably undertake. The boat owner can also usually handle a fracture in the laminate or a hole in the skin about the size of, say, a dinner plate. This represents moderate damage but not so extensive that mold sections must be gotten from the boat's builder or that complex curves must be recreated from nothing.

For purposes of discussion, I will divide this repair section into three parts:

1. Procedures for repair of surface imperfections which do not penetrate the laminate layers.
2. Procedures for repair of defects which pertain to fractures, holes, and eggshell-type breaks that rupture the laminates.
3. Procedures for repair of fractures through the skin which cannot be worked on from inside the hull. Such holes are called "blind holes" and require special techniques for repair.

1. How to Deal with Surface Imperfections
Most surface defects show evidence that the integrity of the gel coat has been destroyed and some material has

been removed. A kind of "Spackling" must be done and then the gel coat layer must be made cosmetically to match as closely as possible to the original. The analogy with Spackle holds for fiberglass fillers and trowel cements. Fillers must be put on with a flexible putty knife in thin layers which are gradually built up, allowed to cure, and then sanded and painted over (see Figure 4). To achieve a smooth surface, various combinations of filler and gel coat will be needed. Perhaps one layer of filler and two of gel coat will do; sometimes three or more layers of gel coat will be needed for proper finish. Common sense will be your guide.

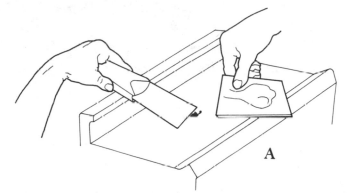

Figure 4. Repairing Damaged Gel Coat. A. *Wipe the damaged area with cloth dampened with acetone. Roughen the gouge with #200 grit paper and wipe again. Mix the new gel coat and patching putty in a 1 : 1 ratio and mix in the catalyst. As shown here, work this mixture into the gouge and press firmly on a putty knife to force out air bubbles. Fill the hole until it is about 1/16" above the undamaged surface.* **B.** *Begin the cure by laying cellophane over the patch to cut off the air (as shown here). In 10 to 15 minutes the patch should feel rubbery. Remove the cellophane and trim the patch with a razor blade; then replace the cellophane and allow the patch to cure completely, about 30 minutes. When totally cured the patch will be slightly below the surface, because of shrinkage during the curing process. Feather the sides of the filled gouge with #200 grit paper and mix pure gel coat with a few drops of catalyst. Deposit a tiny dab of gel coat to about 1/16" above the surface and again cover with cellophane.* **C.** *When the patch is rubbery once more, trim the patch again with a razor blade. Put a dab of colored gel coat on the edge of the patch and cover with cellophane. With a squeegee or a razor blade, spread this dab of gel coat over the patch level with the surrounding surface (shown here). Leave the cellophane on overnight; this will form the finish coat, ready to be sanded smooth.* **D.** *The next day, sand the patch first with #400 grit wet paper and then with #600 grit wrapped around a sanding block. Finally, as shown here, buff the patch several times with carnauba wax and a sheepskin buffing pad.*

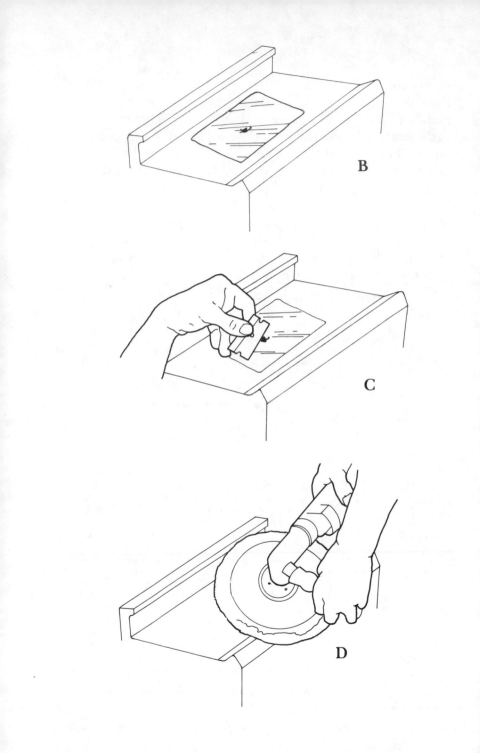

B

C

D

Scrapes and gouges in the surface that are jagged and contain off-abraded material must be cleaned out well if a satisfactory bond with fillers is to be obtained. A rough carbide burr chucked into an electric drill is the best tool for this work. One of the variable-R.P.M. drills works well as you can suit the speed of the tip to the work.

Obtaining a reasonably comparable matching of the gel coat with the original is the most difficult part of surface repairs. Even the boatmaker's supplied gel coat generally varies from batch to batch, and weathering of your hull will make for considerable difference as compared with the supplied gel coat. If you have an artist's eye perhaps you can tint the gel coat with color; if not, you must do the best you can. If that is not good enough, you may have to opt for a complete paint job.

2. *Through-Laminate Punctures*

When punctures and fractures go clear through the laminate layers, the primary consideration is to restore the structural soundness of the hull. There will be no weakness at the repair and the patch will have something close to 100 percent of the strength of the original if properly done.

The first step in repairing such damage is to cut back the stove-in section to sound material. Now sand the edges of the hole with a coarse emery disc to "feather" the edges to receive the new patch material and resin. The width of the feathering should be considerable so that a generous area of rough surface is presented for bonding. Then a patch which functions something like the butt block in a wooden hull is applied on the inside of the hole (and inside the hull). This supplies strength and also a backing form for the subsequent outer patches. The edges of the backed hole are again smoothed with the disc and the depression is filled with mat and cloth to match the original construction. These laminates are sanded smooth and a new gel coating is sprayed or painted on (see Figure 5).

If you have allowed sufficient overlap of the patches and if the resin was applied well, the patch will have more than adequate mechanical and chemical strength. If the new material and the hull are fair, without air bubbles, there will be good mechanical bonding. Bubbles can be prevented by proper squeegeeing of the patch and by pressing the mat strongly with the hands. Try to match exactly the plies in the original—if mat and roving are both used in the original construction, do the same—in the same order—in your patching. Woven roving has a coarse waffle weave and is easily recognized.

Good chemical bonding depends on thorough saturation of the reinforcing material and use of properly catalyzed resin. Mix a small amount of resin following the manufacturer's instructions and make a small test patch on a piece of scrapwood. If the test resin sets up too soon for careful working or too slow to work in a reasonably continuous operation, then the catalyst can be varied in the real job to give optimum working conditions as outlined in the early part of this chapter. If the repair is really tricky, use epoxy resin because of its greater chemical bonding strength.

3. Blind Holes

Holes which cannot be reached from inside the hull are not difficult to repair. An opening sufficient to insert a backing form, usually of cardboard, must be made in the hull. The cardboard is removed and bent to the hull shape as often as necessary to ensure that it is fair. The form is now covered with resin-wet mat

A

Figure 5. Repairing Through-Laminate Punctures. A. *Wipe the area of impact or break with acetone, and use a saber saw or keyhole saw to cut back to the structurally sound part of the hull.* **B.** *On the inside of the hull, feather back around the sawn hole 3" or 4" into the sound fiberglass to create an adequate bonding surface for the patch. A #24 grit disc will cut quickly; a #50 is best for finishing.* **C.** *Use a piece of cardboard covered with cellophane as a backing for the patch. Tape it over the hole on the outside of the hull, allowing a 5" or 6" overlap. (A thin sheet of aluminum is better than cardboard if there are sharp bends in the surface at the location of the hole, as at the sheer-deck line.* **D.** *The fiberglass mat and cloth used for the patch should be 4" or 5" larger than the hole to allow for bonding. First, wet-out the mat with catalyzed resin and apply it over the hole on the inside of the hull. Then do the same with the cloth. Be sure the patches are thoroughly saturated so that no air bubbles or resin-starved areas develop.* **E.** *To apply, lay the saturated patch over the hole and cover it with a sheet of cellophane. With a rubber squeegee, smooth the surface of the patch from the center toward the edges without removing a great deal of resin. Wipe up the excess as you work, and avoid leaving bubbles. Allow the cellophane to remain overnight.* **F.** *The next day, remove the cardboard (or aluminum) backing from the surface of the hull and with the sanding discs feather the outside edges of the hole back 3" or 4".* **G.** *Mask the area on the hull around the hole with light posterboard or oiled paper. Next, build up the depression around the hole by applying layers of fiberglass mat and cloth wetted-out with catalyzed resin until the surface is slightly higher than the surrounding hull surface.* **H.** *During application, the resin should be daubed— not brushed—on to avoid shifting the patch layers and the formation of air bubbles.* **I.** *Cover the new outside patch with cellophane to hasten the curing process. As you did on the inside patch, smooth the surface with a rubber squeegee to compress the patch and spread the resin evenly. Leave the cellophane in place on the patch overnight to set up.* **J.** *When the patch has set up, cut off the excess mat and cloth with a sharp Exacto knife. Then let the patch harden.* **K.** *When the patch has hardened completely, sand the edges of the patch smooth to blend with the surrounding hull surface, using gradually finer sanding discs.* **L.** *Mix the gel coat as it came colored from the manufacturer with catalyst and work it into the patch, filling the weave of the cloth. Cover the patch with cellophane and squeegee it smooth (work from the center out toward the edges, pulling the excess out onto the masking paper). Allow it to cure overnight and then remove the cellophane. Sand the patch first with #400 grit wet paper then with #600 grit wrapped around a sanding block. Finally, buff the patch several times with carnauba wax and a sheepskin buffing pad. (For very large patches, thin the gel coat 1 : 1 with a thinner recommended by the manufacturer and spray it on. After it dries, before spraying the patch again sand the surface of the patch with fine wet-or-dry sandpaper. After spraying the final layer of gel coat, spray on a parting agent recommended by the manufacturer to guarantee curing. When the curing process is complete, buff with a rubbing compound and carnauba wax.)*

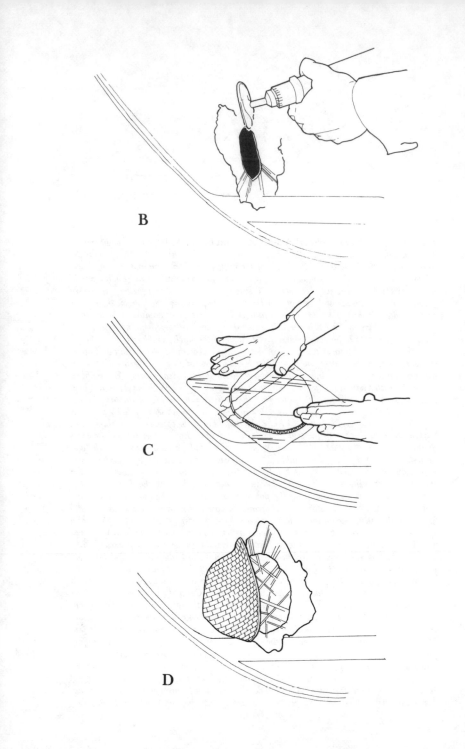

B

C

D

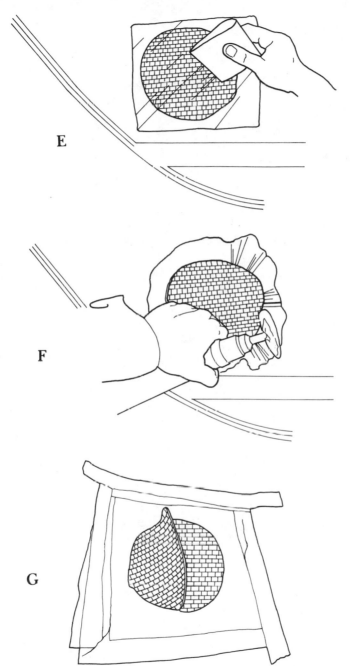

E

F

G

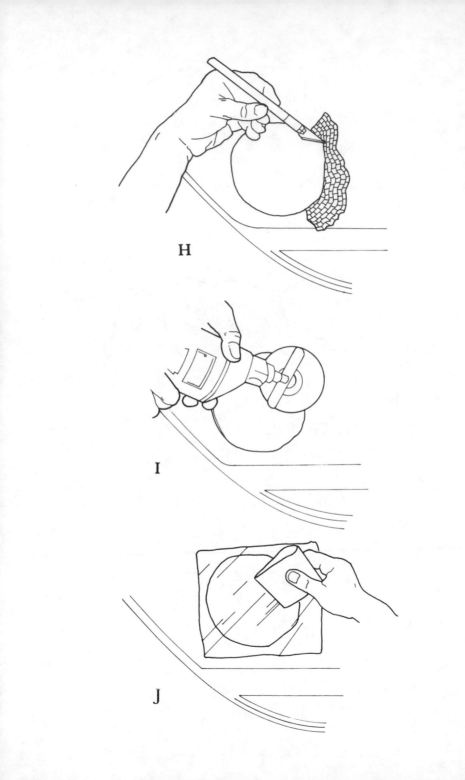

H

I

J

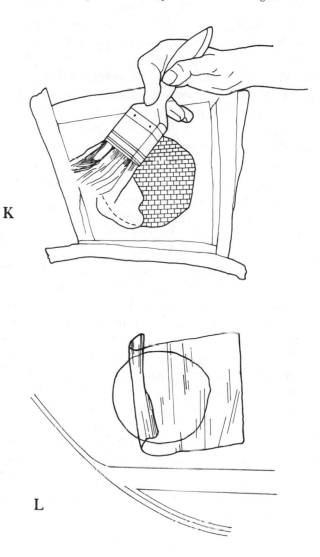

K

L

and wired through the hole to wooden battens as shown in Figure 6. The cardboard and internal patch, after cure, serve as the backup for all additional patches. When the cardboard is inserted for the last time prior to wiring, one should paint resin on the back side. This will prevent dissolving of the cardboard if it gets wet and will prevent its falling into the bilge to clog the pumps. If the blind hole falls on a space that is occupied by a tank, the inner backup form should be thin sheet aluminum or a material compatible with the tank's contents.

ADDITIONS TO FIBERGLASS HULLS

When it is necessary to fasten new cabin fittings to fiberglass hulls, cloth and resin can make attachments sufficiently strong. A shelf, by way of example, is easily attached to a fiberglass hull. This can be done by temporarily securing the wood to the hull with epoxy glue and glassing the joints. If a lot of weight is to be carried by the new attachment, or if it will be subject to stress, then nonrusting screws or through-bolts can be used everywhere but through the hull skin. Many layers of glass and resin should be used when super-strong attachment is necessary. When glassing new work to hulls, the paint on the inside should be removed with a disc sander for proper bonding. Wiping down with an acetone-soaked rag will remove oil or grease and guarantee better adhesion.

No matter what its nature, when making a repair take some time to study the problem and work out the steps that will be necessary. Anticipate difficulties by doing the repair in your head. It is good to undertake the fiberglassing of some small project, like a toolbox, before beginning. Shortcuts and refinements are discovered

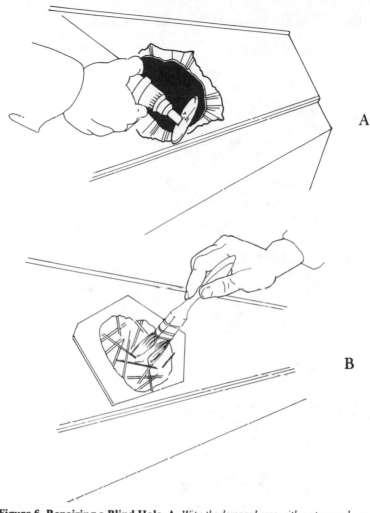

A

B

Figure 6. Repairing a Blind Hole. A. *Wipe the damaged area with acetone and use a saber saw or a keyhole saw to cut back to sound material. Then feather the inside of the hole back for 2" or 3" to form a bonding surface.* **B.** *Cut a piece of cardboard slightly larger than the hole to use as backing for the inside patch (if the hole is in a tank, use thin sheet aluminum instead of cardboard since any liquid in the tank would cause the cardboard to disintegrate). Saturate a mat patch of the proper size with catalyzed resin and lay it on the cardboard backing.* **C.** *Bend thin wires into a "U" shape and insert them through the backing and the saturated mat so that they will be close to the edges of the hole. The wires will exert pressure and hold the backing in place until the inside patch has cured.* **D.** *Insert the backing and saturated mat into the hole so that the mat is pressed against the inside edges of the hole with the wires sticking through the hole. Attach short wood battens to the wires to hold the inside patch firmly in place and let the patch cure overnight. When it has cured, remove the battens and finish the outside patching as with routine impact damage (see Figure 5).*

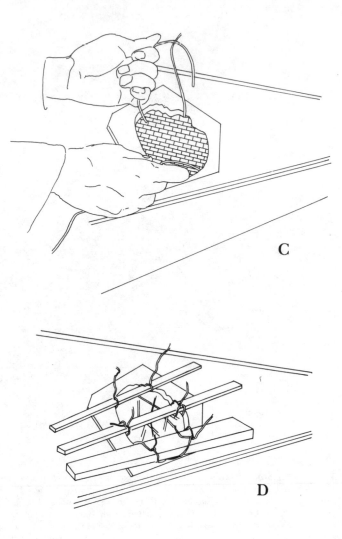

C

D

with a little practice. If a problem is encountered, write the manufacturer of the resin or cloth and explain your needs. Most companies are conscientious about answering.

7. Wood Boats—Construction and Materials

Though fiberglass and, to some extent, aluminum now constitute the major materials of which modern boats are built, we are seeing a renewed interest in wood boats. *Wood Boat* magazine, which concentrates on restoration of classic yachts and new construction in a few specialized yards, has achieved a large circulation. The appearance on the yachting scene of new ultra-light boats racing under various ocean racing rules has sparked a return to an old form of wood boat—the molded-plywood vessel.

In addition there are a great many wood boats still in operation, and owners of such craft seem increasingly interested in devoting time to learning proper maintenance techniques for these beautiful craft to preserve their lives.

In general, two kinds of wood are involved in boat construction: hardwoods like oak and mahogany, and softwoods like spruce and fir. Each of these woods has properties that make it better for one use or another. The hardwoods make better structural members like keel, frames, deadwood, and stem, while the softwoods make better planking and decks.

Trees grow by adding new concentric circles called "annual rings." How the saw blade intercepts these rings determines the nature of the lumber that is extracted. If the saw blade cuts the log on a tangent, the boards are called "slash" or "plain sawed". If the blade cuts the log on a radius, the planks are called "quarter" or "rift sawed." For repairing boats, the lumber's grain direction is extremely important. Slash-grain or plain-sawed lumber is best for planking; decking is best quarter sawed. Boards tend to shrink almost twice as much when plain sawed as quarter sawed. For this reason all lumber, and especially planking lumber, should be *air-*dried to about 18 percent moisture content before use in boats. These days it is increasingly difficult to obtain decent lumber of any kind. On the other hand we now are seeing a rebirth of dedicated craftsmen who are proud of their trade and who are putting together small sawmills, selecting and getting out trees, sawing and curing fine lumber. If you are fortunate enough to live near one of these mills, take the time to visit and find out what woods are available that are suitable for boat repair.

BOAT WOOD AT THE PRESENT TIME

Boat wood in suitable species and lengths is becoming almost impossible to obtain, but this does not mean the end of wood boats. Methods for laminating large timbers for deadwood, keel, and frames of small boats are well developed. Chemical treatment of less rot-resistant woods like Douglas fir are also standard today. And designs for molded-plywood and Douglas fir sheet plywood are proliferating.

SOME PLANKING METHODS

It will be useful to discuss briefly the ways in which wood is used as the skin of waterborne craft. The most common of these is called "carvel," which may be a corruption of the word "caravel," meaning a smooth-planked naval or commercial vessel. Carvel planking is fastened to frames or "ribs" with the edges butted together to form a tight seam. Fastenings used can be wooden trunnels, galvanized nails, square-cut boat nails, copper rivets, serrated alloy nails, and alloy screws. The watertightness of carvel planking is a factor of the quality of the seam. A caulking of cotton wicking is generally driven into a "vee" seam of carvel planking to make a tight seam. With carvel planking the interior seam must be tight or the caulking exits through the seam and leaks will result. Carvel planking is the easiest to repair by removing the old plank (strake) and fitting a new one. Sometimes double carvel planking is laid, where two skins are fitted one on top of the other, the seams of one falling between the seams of the other, but this is rare today.

Lapstrake or "clinker" planking designates a method where a small portion of one plank is laid or "lapped" over the other and fastened, usually with copper rivets and burrs. This method of construction produces a strong, lightweight, and easily propelled craft. Many of last century's rowing boats, the so-called sea skiffs, and the great Viking longboats were planked in this manner. The famous "Whitehall" rowing boats that chandlers, ferrymen, and crimps used on the waterfronts of the world were lapstrake built. Some of these designs can be seen in maritime museums, and they are spectacular for their fine lines and beauty.

Boat owners should be able to recognize different

plank fastenings because they are a clue to how the boat is constructed. Lapstrake planking is difficult to repair and requires a high order of woodworking craftsman-ship.

Care should be taken when storing lapstrake boats ashore. The single greatest source of trouble with this class of craft occurs when the boat dries out and the seams open up. Debris falls into the seams, and when the boat is relaunched the planks are prevented from closing properly no matter how long it is afloat. Several seasons of this treatment can ruin the staunchest lapstrake craft. Most of the older boats that are of this construction and still in good condition have been regularly stored afloat. If small lapstrake craft are stored ashore for the winter, they should be stored inside under conditions of high humidity and protected from the sun and drying winds. One technique is to line them with old rugs and burlap and to hose down or otherwise wet out the boat at regu-lar intervals.

Synthetic rubber and Thiokol compounds are being used in new lapstrake construction and promise some relief from opening seams. The elasticity of these com-pounds permits the seams to open and close without rupture of the seam line, thereby preventing foreign matter from entering.

STRIP PLANKING

Strip planking is especially adapted to amateur building because compound curves can easily be planked up with-out the necessity for "lining off" as is done by profes-sionals. In essence the technique calls for strips, either convex and concave so they can be "rolled" around the frames or else bevelled so each strip can be offset, to be laid one on top of the other with glue between. The fastenings are generally nails driven and set with a countersink. A great deal of labor is involved in strip planking, but the ease with which inexperienced builders can plank up is generally considered worth it. After planking, temporary molds which are set on the stations to develop shape are removed and frames are either steam-bent in or laminated cold with epoxy glue. Repairs are made in strip-planked boats by cutting out the hole or puncture with a nail-cutting blade in a power saw. The bad sections are removed with a floor-cutting chisel or a ripping hammer, and new strips are glued and edge-nailed in. Few examples of strip-planked boats will be encountered by the boat owner.

MOLDED PLYWOOD

Though molded plywood has been used extensively for many years in the production of small boats such as dinghies, except for military high-speed craft like PT boats it had not been used for medium or large pleasure craft. In the past few years, however, this has changed, and we have seen ultra-light sailboats winning many of the ocean-racing classics, and many of these boats are of molded-plywood construction. The advantage of molded plywood has to do with the concept of "stressed-skin" or monocoque construction. Molded-plywood boats are made by laying up layer after layer of thin veneer in a suitable adhesive. Heated molds are utilized by some manufacturers with air bags or matched dies to exert heat and pressure on the charged mold quite similar to molded fiberglass techniques.

The resulting hull is watertight, strong, impact-resistant, and extremely light for the mass of the material. A further advantage of "stressed-skin" construction is that reinforcing "ribs" or frames can be dispensed with thwartships, and longitudinal strength is provided by bulkheads and compartmenting. This cuts down considerably on the total hull weight. Aircraft of the World War I era were often made of molded plywood for this reason. The disadvantage of molded plywood for the amateur owner is the difficulty in repairing punctures and holes.

MARINE PLYWOOD

Because of its extreme versatility and the refinement of manufacturing techniques which turn out an excellent product, plywood has come to assume an important role in boatbuilding. A major fault of older plywood—the delamination of the plies under certain conditions—has been virtually eliminated with the development of 100 percent waterproof glues.

The Douglas Fir Plywood Association oversees quality control and issues standards for the member lumber mills. Plywood consists of an odd number of layers of veneer sliced from a turning log. The log is placed in a special lathe and very sharp knives peel the layers off in precision thicknesses.

The layers are laid up so that the grain of one layer runs at 90° angles to the next, and then bonded with waterproof glues, heat, and pressure. By alternating the direction of the grain in successive plies, maximum advantage is taken of laminate strength.

IMPORTANCE OF PLYWOOD GRADES

Two major distinctions of plywood as manufactured are whether it is an *interior* or *exterior* grade. Waterproof glue is not used in interior plywood, and it should never be purchased for use in boats for any application whatever. Because of the high humidity and heat, even inside the cabin of a small boat plies are likely to delaminate. On the other hand exterior plywood is fabricated with water-proof glue and should be used for interior joinerwork, as well as deck structures, seats, and on or about the deck. If you obtain remnants of plywood cut from a whole sheet, be certain that it is exterior grade, as sometimes the grade marks have been cut off. It is pointless to waste valuable time building something that will come apart later.

It is possible to save money by choosing a grade of exterior plywood which has small defects on the outside when the surface will not be seen. Though not suitable for finish work, lesser grades are perfectly adequate for decking or cabin sole which will later be covered by canvas or carpeting.

Plywood grade and type is identified by marks burned into the edges or stamped with indelible ink. Tables 3 and 4, supplied by the Douglas Fir Plywood Association, show trademarks, grades, veneer qualities, core construction, and available panel sizes suitable for boat-building with all glues 100 percent waterproof.

By choosing core quality and veneer grade commensurate with the finished work, savings can be effected. When only one side will show, for instance in cabin flooring, an A-A grade (good both sides) would be needlessly over qualitied. For planking and planking repairs, it is just the reverse; Marine Grade A-A should always be used. Only the boat's skin keeps the sea outside, and for this reason planking should be the finest obtainable. Planking is subjected to considerable stress in making the bends required to curve around frames. In use, the skin receives countless blows against docks and floating debris. Therefore economy-grade panels with voids in the core and patches in the surface veneer should not be used for planking. Water will enter the channels formed by core voids and destroy paint, the veneers will rupture at the core voids, and patches are prone to popping out.

Table 3
Grades of Plywood for Boatbuilding[a]

Grade-Trademark	Typical Uses in Boatbuilding	Veneer Quality			Thickness Available
		FACE	BACK	CORES	
MARINE-EXT-DFPA	May be used for *any* marine application.	A	A	*	Available in standard sizes and thicknesses. Also factory spliced long lengths.
		A	B	*	
		B	B	*	
EXT-DFPA. A-A	Planking, bulkheads, superstructure, and decks. Also cabin joinerwork where finished bright and appearance of both sides is important.	A	A	C	same
EXT-DFPA. A-B	An alternate for Grade A-A for all uses where the appearance of only one side is important, such as in cabin roofing one side of which will be painted or canvas covered.	A	B	C	same
EXT-DFPA PLYSHIELD	Use where appearance of one side only is important and where voids in the coring are not important, such as cabin sole flooring, or interior joiner work which will be painted.	A	C	C	same
EXT-DFPA PLYFORM	Can be used in any application where canvas, linoleum, or heavy paint will cover, as both surfaces are imperfect, and where structural strength of the core is unimportant, such as berth tops, cabinet shelves.	B	B	C	5/8 3/4

*All cores are specially constructed without voids for marine use.
[a]Courtesy of the Douglas Fir Plywood Association.

Table 4
Veneer Qualities
Used in Douglas Fir Plywood*

Veneer Quality	Defect Limitation
A	Presents smooth surface. Free from knots, open splits, pitch-pockets, and other open defects.
	Veneer shall be well joined if more than one piece is used.
	Admits discoloration, sapwood, and pitch streaks, averaging not more than ⅜″ width and blending with color of wood.
	Admits maximum of 18 veneer patches in 4′ × 8′ sheet.
	Admits shims and neatly made panel patches.
	Shims may not be used over or around any type of patch and multiple repairs must be limited to *two* patches.
	All patches and repairs to run parallel to the grain.
	Admits approved plastic filler in splits and other minor defects up to $\frac{1}{32}$″ in width; in small splits or openings up to $\frac{1}{16}$″ in width if not more than 2″ long; in small chipped areas or openings not to exceed ⅛″ wide by ¼″ long.
B	Presents solid surface. Free from open defects except splits not wider than $\frac{1}{32}$″.
	Vertical borer holes permitted if not exceeding $\frac{1}{16}$″ in diameter and averaging not more than 1 per sq. ft.; and also horizontal tunnels $\frac{1}{16}$″ across, 1″ length, 12 in number in 4′ × 8′ panel, or proportionately in other dimensions.
C Repaired	For underlayment grade only. Tight knots up to 1½″ in greatest dimension and worm and borer holes or other open defects not to exceed ¼″ and ½″ allowed.
	Splits—not to exceed $\frac{1}{16}$″ wide allowed.
	Solid, tight pitch-pockets, ruptured and torn grain, minor sanding defects and sander skips up to 5% of panel area admitted.
C	Knotholes—1″ in least dimension.
	Pitch-pockets—not wider than 1″.
	Splits—³⁄₁₆″ (must taper to point).
	Worm or borer holes ⅝″ × 1½″.
	Tight knots—1½″.
	Plugs, patches, shims, and minor sanding defects admitted.

*Courtesy of the Douglas Fir Plywood Association.

Plywood has made possible stronger wood boats, with less weight and greater rot resistance, than run-of-the-mill lumber. Plywood is an excellent and versatile material, but it should be used within its limitations. Plywood edge grain must be well sealed with paint, sealer, or fiberglass-reinforced plastic because the edges are vulnerable and will absorb water through capillary action. By its very nature plywood presents large areas of thin veneer to the weather and sun. This causes many short checks parallel to the grain. It is an extremely difficult task to fill these checks properly and achieve a smooth surface once the weathering process has begun. Checking can be minimized by sealing the surface well when the panel is new. Several coats of a stock plywood sealer like Firzite or a well-thinned marine paint undercoat should be used. In between coats the sealer must be allowed to dry well and be sanded.

Most plywood manufacturers also make panels faced with oak, mahogany, birch, maple, walnut, or other rare woods for interior use. These panels are useful where the wood can be finished bright (varnished) and where the natural beauty of the wood will enhance the work. Panels overlaid and impregnated with resin are also available; these positively eliminate checking and weathering. Such panels, though slightly more expensive, are excellent for decks and cabin tops. Before you buy plywood, be sure you are able to recognize the genuine marine article by grade and type (see Tables 3 and 4).

HULL SHAPE IN WOOD BOATS

The round-bottom hull is the most common hull shape in American boat design. It is a shape which has good buoyancy and good hydrodynamic performance, and permits designers to pack more accommodation into a given size than with most other configurations. Within

the class of "round bottom" are many variations, ranging from a full dinghy shape to the sleek wine-glass or
fin-keel types. Repairs to round-bottom boats require
handiness with tools and some knowledge of steam-
bending techniques, which will be discussed in a later
chapter.

V-bottom or hard-chine boats are good performers
under both power and sail. Harry Pidgeon's famous yawl
Islander that he sailed around the world was a V-bottom
type. Many of the "cathedral"-hulled planing motor-
boats are deadrise V-bottomed. Because of the flatter
planing surface on the water, V-bottom boats are almost
always faster for a given length and horsepower than
round-bottom craft of the same general kind. Sometimes
one will find boats that are a combination of V and round
bottom with the V forward and the round aft. Large
cabin cruisers designed for high planing speeds are often
built in this configuration.

Flat-bottom boats are traditional for small working
craft. The rowboat or skiff is the most prolific example
of the type. Flat-bottom boats are easy to haul, easy to
build, and good performers if waves are not the breaking
variety. Dories, New Haven sharpies, and duck boats are
examples of wholesome flat-bottom working craft. Ches-
apeake Bay oyster boats and bugeyes are examples of
large working craft built to flat-bottom configuration.
Both power and sail have been used to propel such craft.
Retractable centerboards or leeboards are used to prevent falling off to leeward.

An advantage of small tenders built with a flat bottom
is that a single sheet of plywood can often be used to
plank the bottom, making for strong, seamless, watertight construction. The major drawback of flat-bottom
boats is their tendency to pound in rough water. Phil
Bolger, for one, has designed offshore sport-fishing

boats with some rocker in the bottom which lessens this tendency.

These, then, are the hull classifications that all wooden boats will conform to.

8. Wood-Boat Maintenance

Wood boats mainly of stressed-skin, monocoque, or molded-plywood construction are being built today. Some specialized yards are also turning out traditional designs in wood on a custom basis. But by far the biggest interest in wood at present lies in maintaining older wood boats and in restoring classic yachts. Indeed, classic yacht restoration has become the most prestigious activity in yachting today.

This is fortunate, for without the time and money spent by these dedicated owners, many of the fine craft that have contributed to America's sea tradition would have disappeared from the scene. Instead, new techniques have overcome the scarcity of certain woods, and new organizations like Wood Boats of Norwalk, Connecticut, have developed techniques for preserving and restoring classic craft.

The primary objective in preserving the structural integrity of the wood boat is to maintain the surface coatings that protect it from weathering and deterioration. If weathering is allowed to proceed, breakdown of fastenings, rot, loosening of planking, and rusted ironwork will result in an unseaworthy hull. It is routine care and maintenance while in operation that will best keep a boat alive. In this chapter I will formulate principles for good vessel maintenance and discuss what to look for in a well-cared-for vessel.

WOOD PLANKING

Planking surface gives little trouble unless it is smashed against something or the paint film breaks down. Checks or cracks sometimes appear spontaneously in planks, but this is generally a phenomenon of a new boat. As settling-in and hull working stabilize, such "builder's" defects will be repaired and no longer be a problem.

While you are inspecting hull planking, observe the hood ends of the planking at the bow and stern where they lay against the rabbets. Frequently the tapering of the planks necessitates the ends being quite narrow. Splits sometimes appear in the way of the fastenings which are often driven very close together. Butt blocks which join two planks between frames should be checked for splits and to be sure fastenings are secure. Unfairness in planking in the region of the butt is a sign of butt-block trouble. Even if it is necessary to open up sections of the interior ceiling, it is wise to provide for easy access to butt blocks for ongoing inspection. How to check and replace fastenings in butt blocks and planking will be treated in the next chapter.

CHECK THE FASTENINGS

The key to keeping the structural integrity of a wooden boat lies in the nature and condition of the fastenings. A wood boat is a collection of thousands of individual pieces of wood. The fastenings hold it all together.

Carvel planking is the most common sheathing you

will find. Fastenings in this construction will be galvanized boat nails, galvanized screws, Monel screws or nails, silicon-bronze or "Everdur" screws, or "Anchorfast" serrated nails. In the heyday of wooden boatbuilding galvanized screws were of exceptional quality, made of Swedish iron with threads well cut and hot-dip galvanizing applied after machining. The same applied to the square-cut galvanized boat nails.

Today such traditional fastenings, unless found as a treasure in someone's basement, are no longer available. A worthless substitute, the electroplated galvanized fastening, has appeared. It has a thin, short-lasting coating and should not be used in boat work. Such fastenings should be replaced with Monel or silicon-bronze as a matter of routine.

When your boat is hauled, go over her carefully and look at each row of fastenings. Look closely at the bungs (also called plugs) for rust stains or weeping. Look to see if the bung heads are slightly above the surface of the plank. If the bungs are not level with the surrounding surface, it is probable that oxidation of the fastening is lifting the bung slightly. If there is a rust stain, then it is certain that the head of the fastening has begun to break down. Rust means that the zinc protective coating of the screw or boat nail has deteriorated and the fastening is oxidizing. Bad fastenings should be marked with a crayon or magic marker so that none will be overlooked.

Plugs rise above the surrounding surface because rust accumulates under the wood plug, gradually loosening it and forcing it up. The portion of the fastening into the frame is usually also affected and holding power is lessened. An evaluation of the fastening shank must be made by removing at least one or two fastenings. Superficial defects like weeping and raised bungs are often the clue to a more serious structural defect.

When all the bad bungs and fastenings have been circled, take a sharp ¼-inch wood chisel and carefully chip out the bung a little at a time, being careful not to break down the edges of the hole as this will make seating a new plug difficult. When the plug is out, take an icepick, a small screwdriver, or a chisel and scrape the head of the fastening to see what it's made of. Rust means it's a galvanized screw or boat nail; if it's a screw, further probing should turn up signs of a slot.

If the outlines of a slot appear, there is a chance that the screw can be withdrawn. Keep cleaning out the slot as much as you can. Next, a screwdriver bit should be chucked into a stout ratchet brace. The bit should make a perfect fit into the screw slot because any slip will damage the walls of the slot and full torsion on the screw head will not be possible. If necessary, a slightly oversize bit should be ground down to fit. Grind the sides of the bit flat—that is, remove the taper—so the blade surfaces are parallel to match the parallel surfaces of the slot. To remove the screw, place the bit in the slot and lean heavily against the end knob of the brace. Make the first turn to *drive the screw farther in,* not to back it out. This will often break the seal and loosen the screw so that it can be backed out. Use the ratchet for greater torque and don't let the blade slip out of the slot. Even if difficult, it should be possible to remove at least one or two fastenings to evaluate the condition of the fastenings in general. Sometimes fastenings will be good in one area of the planking and not in another, so different areas of the planking should be tested.

Probably the best indicator of fastening condition is the contour of the planking itself. If the planks are bulged outward between the seams or have a so-called pumpkin look, then this is a pretty sure sign that the fastenings are no longer holding. A broken or cracked paint line at the seams or protruding caulking indicates excessive working of the planks. The usual reason for this is that the fastenings are no longer holding the planks securely. Refastening with screws or boat nails placed alongside the original is the remedy for this condition.

If there is rust and weeping at the bung but the planking remains fair and there is no evidence of excessive seam working, you can assume that the part of the fastening into the frame is still good and holding. It is probable that only the head is rusting. A cleaning and sealing of the fastening will usually be sufficient to cure the problem. This is done by removing the bung and scraping the fastening to remove flaked rust. A carbide burr smaller than the bung hole should be chucked into a variable-speed electric drill and touched lightly against the head of the fastening. Be sure the burr is much smaller in diameter than the hole or the walls will be damaged. If the head is the rounded one of a boat nail, a cupped-end burr should be used. Exert enough pressure so that the drill does not slip. When you have cleaned the head in this manner, mark the fastening so you know it is done, and move on to attack the next one.

After all weeping fastenings have been derusted, mix up a small quantity of epoxy resin and catalyst. With a small camel hair artist's brush, daub the head of the nail or screw with the mixture. Be sure the activated resin covers all the head of the fastening so air is sealed off. With a clean cloth, wipe off the excess resin. It is a good idea to have new bungs ready for insertion and to have an assistant working alongside you replacing them and giving them a tap with a mallet as you go along.

For oxidized fastenings, it is my opinion that catalyzed resin makes a much better rust preventive and sealer than Rustoleum, zinc chromate, or red lead. These old standbys are still fine for ironwork, but a more tenacious and chemically bonding preparation is needed for troublesome fastenings. The epoxy helps to overcome sloughing-off of rust and stops continuing deterioration. The epoxy does not leach off like paint: it keeps a hard, ceramic-like coating between the metal and air and water. The extended cure for weeping fastenings that is possible with this method is well worth the extra labor, expense, and trouble of working with catalyzed resin.

When routinely replacing plugs, epoxy is ideal if the hole walls have been damaged or lost their clean wall contours because the epoxy will act as an adhesive and will flow into and fill the voids between the plug and the hole. New plugs, of course, should be placed with the grain running in the same direction as the planking grain. When the glue has hardened, the excess plug should be cut off a little at a time to test the grain. A very sharp wood chisel placed against the plug and lightly struck with the heel of the hand works well. Use only a wooden or rubber-faced mallet to seat new plugs, and tap lightly, for if you whack too hard or use a metal hammer the wood will compress and after the boat is painted and launched the plugs will swell up and protrude, breaking the paint film. The whole job will have to be done again if this happens. Chem-Tech T-88 or two-part resorcinol glue are best for seating plugs in new work or where plugs and holes are both in good condition.

Sometimes probing will reveal a fastening that is completely eaten away and an ice pick or awl goes right into the frame. This is an indication that the boat is undergoing severe galvanic corrosion. Now is the time to check the polarity of electrical equipment and engine ground to make sure no strong electrical currents are eating away the fastenings. If necessary, one of the impressed-current electrical devices to neutralize stray currents should be considered.

If fastenings are so bad that a complete refastening is called for, treat the old fastening heads as described with epoxy and drive a new fastening in alongside the old one. The best practice is to use a Monel nail or screw so that action between dissimilar metals does not occur. Even if the old fastening is a galvanized boat nail, drive a screw next to it when doing a major refastening. At one time I felt it permissible to use a silicon-bronze or Everdur screw next to a deteriorated galvanized fastening. My reasoning told me that deterioration of the old fastening had already occurred, that the current flowed to the more noble metal as a cathode, and that the galvanic effect would therefore be minimal. I no longer believe that this is the correct course to take. Mixing of dissimilar metals is a risky business at best, and the rapidly declining number of classic wooden boats in existence warrants the expenditure of a slight bit of money to guarantee survival. I think that now I would contact one of the manufacturers of bolts and screws (Southern Screw is one that comes to mind) and purchase Monel screws in the needed sizes. When one is completely refastening, the number of screws needed is fairly large and many manufacturers will sell directly to the customer if the quantity is sufficient. The increased risk of stray current corrosion is vastly greater today with the proliferation of electronic navigating and communications equipment placed aboard even small cruisers, so take this into account when purchasing new fastenings.

PREBORE FOR EVERYTHING

In order that the wood not split when expansion and contraction take place, it is essential that lead holes be bored for all fastenings in boat work. When refastening is done the boat has usually been hauled and the wood is dry, and when the boat is refloated the fibers will swell. This places pressure against the fastening and will cause checking and splitting of planking ends if there is no space for expansion. Preboring relieves the fibers around the screw so swelling will not cause splitting. When boring for a nail, a single drill bit slightly under the thickness of the nail is sufficient, but three separate holes must be drilled as pilot holes for screws. The first of these is for the point of the screw and ensures that the screw is driven where you want it to go; the second is for the middle of the threads about halfway up the screw; the third is for a snug fit around the threadless shank. In addition, provision must be made for countersinking the screw head in flat- or oval-headed screws, and for a wooden plug if bungs are used to cover the fastening. Major tool manufacturers now make patent counterbores which will do part or all of this necessary preboring in one operation.

Before you undertake the actual work, make some test borings and drive a few screws into scrap lumber of the same kind as you will later be fastening. Sticking the screws into softened brown laundry soap pressed into an empty sardine can will lubricate the threads and make driving easier. Professionals use a Yankee ratchet screwdriver to drive the screws almost home and then finish with a heavy-duty brace chucked with a screwdriver bit. Be sure the bit is a perfect fit or you will damage the walls of the screw slot. You will be able to tell by feel when the screw is tight enough and stop at this point or the screwhead will be wrung off and you must either leave it or go to great trouble to remove it and start again. As the screw bites, you should be able to see the plank draw in and the luting compound squeeze out of the seam. The boat owner should purchase plug cutters for the most popular sizes of screws because it is rarely possible to buy plugs of the right size and wood species when you need them. Patent plugs cutters are usually found in the catalogs of marine dealers and tool manufacturers such as the Stanley Company.

How to Deal with Seams and Caulking

Unless the seams are relieved with a shallow groove, as in the method called "graved" planking, carvel planking is generally smooth at the seams. In order to maintain the unbroken paint coating at the seams it is necessary that there be no excessive working at the seam and that the seams themselves be perfectly stopped and filled. When working with a new boat having brand-new fastenings, frames, and planks, this perfection is possible. But the older boat, both power and sail, will "work" in a seaway and small movements at the seams will take place. I have felt that overemphasis on an unbroken paint line at the seams is pointless. The feeling of being "alive" that some vessels have is in part derived from their working. As long as the seams are watertight and the caulking is not forced out, the caulking is doing its job.

For wooden boat owners, improvements in the elastomeric sealants have significantly changed this matter of keeping seams tight. In spite of swelling and shrinking of the wood as it is wet and dried out, a nearly perfect seam caulking that will allow for this is now available. The elastomerics are a synthetic rubber with superior waterproofing qualities, good adhesion to most woods, and a superior elasticity that will last for the life of the boat.

If your boat will require major refitting, including work on the seams, then it is well worth the effort to remove the old seam cement and cotton caulking, and to replace them with new cotton and a Thiokol elastomeric sealant. If you are going to wood-down your hull to remove built-up paint layers, this is a perfect time to change the caulking as well.

The first step in recaulking with elastomerics is to remove and thoroughly clean out the old caulking. For this purpose a seam scraper is necessary. The scraper should be a close fit to the width of the seam and as deep as the compound, that is to say, to the top of the cotton caulk-ing. It is impossible to purchase suitable seam scrapers and they are usually homemade. If you have one of the old heavy steel beer-can openers ("churchkey"), these make ideal seam tools. Grind each side of the point to fit the seam you will be working on. If seam width varies, then make up two or three scrapers in graduated sizes and change them as needed. To get more leverage, tack-weld on a short iron bar, or drill and bolt on a wooden handle. Using a disc sander, hit the seams lightly with a medium disc to outline the limits of the seam. Now use the seam tool with a motion that digs the putty out to-ward you and then lightly scrape back and forth. After all the seam compound is out, wire-brush the dust and dirt out of the opening. If your brush is too wide, shape it by cutting out some of the wire bristles with a pair of wire cutters.

Reefing Seams
The next step is to remove the old cotton caulking if this is found to be necessary. If the old caulking is clean, tight, and unrotted, it is permissible to prime the cotton and lay the elastomeric in on top. If it is not suitable, then the old cotton must be removed and new caulking driven before filling the seams with elastomeric.

If the decision is made to remove the old cotton, it will be necessary to make a "reefing iron." Hooking-out old seams is called "reefing" and the tool used is a "reefing iron." In the old days reefing irons were available in all sizes at the chandlers, but today they will have to be made. To do this, get a long-handled screwdriver of good quality, preferably with a wooden handle, and put a bend into the shank and head till it is in the shape of a question mark (?). The bend should lie in the same plane as the blade (see Figure 7) so that it goes into the seam with the handle parallel to the seam. A good ma-

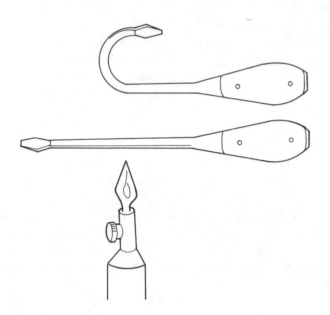

Figure 7. Making a Reefing Iron. *A reefing iron is used to remove the caulking from a small boat's seams. Since it is virtually impossible to buy one, you can make your own. Take a long-handled screwdriver of good quality, preferably with a wooden handle, and with a torch, heat the shank about a third of the way back from the blade tip. When hot, place the screwdriver in a vise and hammer the shank into the shape of a question mark ("?"). Then plunge it into cold water to restore the temper and grind the tip to fit the seam.*

chine shop or blacksmith can make this bend for you and then put the temper back into the blade. When the bend is made, the blade of the new tool can be ground on an emery wheel to the most efficient shape as determined by trial and error for hooking out the cotton. After the cotton is all out, brush the seams and go over them with a vacuum cleaner to remove dust and compound granules.

The new cotton caulking must now be driven. Cotton, when used with elastomeric sealants, serves a purpose somewhat different from in the past. The firmly packed cotton caulking makes the individual planks rigid by act-ing as a wedging between the edges. This limits the working of the plank. At the same time the cotton fills up the gap so that less elastomeric sealant will have to be used. Sealant is expensive and it performs best when the depth of the elastomeric is about half to two-thirds the depth of the seam. This depth allows for best cure and best performance of the synthetic rubber.

A few of the elastomerics, usually those having a poly-sulfide base, require priming the seams with a special liquid before putty-knifing in the compound. I think that priming, unless specifically prohibited by the manufacturer's recommendations, should be applied in all cases. This is because the priming gives better grip to the cotton and improves chemical bond to the old wood. If the brand of elastomeric you are using does not come with a primer, write to the manufacturer and request the name of a suitable primer.

Cotton Caulking

Caulking as the master shipwrights did it is a dead art. The boatyards of today do what you can do—they use common sense and care, and often turn out a decent job. When properly driven, cotton caulking resembles a rope strand about half the size of clothesline for a boat of about 50 feet. It must be tight in order that, when the wood swells, a light groove is compressed into the upper and lower plank edges. At the same time there must not be so much caulking that the swelling forces the planks apart. When the pressure becomes too great, the fastenings are ruptured or the caulking is forced out.

To caulk as it was done by shipwrights, follow this method:

Open the hank, where you will find many strands. Lay the strands out their full length on a clean board of sufficient length. An end containing one, two, or three strands should be gathered up between the palms and rolled with a great deal of pressure to give a tight twist to the strands so you end up with something like a rope. Now you have several balls with different numbers of strands and different thicknesses. Next, choose the ball with just the right number of strands to fill the seam with the proper amount of cotton. The "right" amount will fill the seam to about half to two-thirds of the seam depth when driven home with a caulking iron and light blows of a mallet. The proper size iron is one of a thickness such that it can only enter the seam about half to two-thirds of the depth. With an iron of this size there is no danger that you will inadvertently drive the cotton right through the seam and out the other side. After the cotton has been inserted with the straight iron, a "making" iron which is slightly thicker than the plain iron is used to seat the cotton and compact it. Care must be taken with an older boat that too much cotton not be inserted and driven so hard that it exits through the inside of the plank.

When you use elastomeric sealants it is not necessary to caulk boat seams as tightly as with conventional caulking. This is because it is the elastomeric that prevents water from entering—the cotton merely serves the function of backing up the sealant so an excessive amount is not used and there is something for the bottom of the sealant to bond to. This sounds complicated, but it is quite easily understood by looking at Figure 8. When elastomerics are used, the entrance of water as a result of inexpert caulking is no longer a serious factor.

It will help your work if your irons are kept rust-free and burnished with fine emery, then oiled to keep the cotton from sticking to the metal. A small tuft of cotton should be left protruding from the seam as you come to the end of a strand so that you will know where to take up again. Also, use mallets of different weights to be sure you do not drive the cotton through the seam. Lighter

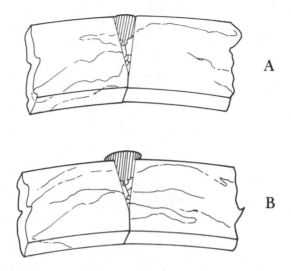

Figure 8. Caulking a Seam with Elastomeric Sealants. *The caulking should be much lighter with elastomeric sealants than when cotton and conventional seam compounds are used. The elastomeric provides the watertightness; the cotton only provides a backing. Priming the seam will further enhance the quality of the sealant's bond.* **A.** *A few strands of cotton are loosely driven to provide a backing for the elastomeric seam filler.* **B.** *Too much cotton driven too tightly will force the sealant outward when the dry planks swell.*

mallets and more care will be needed in softwood planking. Remember, with some practice you will acquire a feel for this work, and with a feel and common sense you will do a creditable job.

Another tip which will prove useful is that the longer a hull has been out of water and dried out, the lighter it should be caulked. The reason for this is that when refloated it will swell more than a boat with a slightly higher moisture content. When making or seating the cotton, be sure that the iron is held level with the seam. If the blade crosses the cotton fibers at an angle, the strands will be ruptured.

If you find that the seam you are caulking is open on the inside of the hull, do not adopt the expedient of fastening a batten inside at the seam between the frames and then caulking against this. As the seam contracts and expands with absorption of moisture, the batten will rupture. This will permit caulking to come out and a dangerous leak could ensure. A much better practice is to make a strip wedge with the bevel all on one side and to glue it in place with one of the superior epoxy glues like Chem-Tech T-88. The strip should be gotton out on a good table saw and then firmly but lightly driven into the seam from the inside. After the glue has set, the strip can be planed flush with a small scrub plane and sanded with a disc sander. Short of replacing the opened strake, this is the best method of closing a troublesome seam.

Elastomeric Caulking

When the cotton is properly imbedded in the seam, preparation may be made for filling with elastomeric compound. Clean-up will be more convenient if the edges of the seam are masked with easily removed masking tape; it is much more difficult if no tape is used and the rubber is permitted to cure.

With deck seams, the cartridge-and-gun method for filling is the quickest. Viscosity of cartridge sealant is more runny than with the knifing types—it is very difficult to keep it from sagging out of topsides or bottom seams—so for these sections be sure to purchase the thicker compound and put it in with a putty knife. A palette may be made from a piece of clean, thin plywood. A lump of compound may be placed on the palette with a spoon. For two-part mixtures, the catalyst may now be worked in following the directions on the can.

Use a good putty knife with a thin, flexible blade to pick up a bead of compound on the tip and press it into the seam firmly. Use enough pressure on the blade so that air bubbles will be forced out. The next time you load the blade, slightly overlap the section you have just finished so that the voids are filled without entrapping air. If the blade of the knife is held diagonal to the seam it is more difficult for bubbles to form under the sealant. It is extremely important that tools not become soiled with sealant or the work will suffer. Wash tools with solvent when they become dirty, and *always* replace the lid on the can between loadings.

A factor to be considered in using elastomeric sealants is whether or not they will be painted over. Many of the silicone-base sealants will not hold paint well. If you are in doubt, it is advisable to use a polysulfide compound which does hold paint well, or else check with the manufacturer for a statement of the product's paint-holding characteristics. Before starting the major work, it is a good idea to run a complete test on a noncritical project, taking it all the way through from preparation and applying the sealant to final sanding and painting. In this way you can debug the program and assure success.

Again, be sure to remove the masking tape before the sealant has set up hard. Also, only fill the seams flush, as the sealant tends to expand in cure. After the sealant has set up you can trim any protruding rubber with a sharp razor blade. Elastomeric seam compounds have significantly reduced work and year-to-year problems of planking seam maintenance. You will find it well worth the expense and effort of changing to this method of caulking.

Maintaining the Keel Assembly

The large timbers in a wooden boat that form the keel, stem, deadwood, horn timber, and shaft log are those structural members which are referred to as the "backbone assembly."

Knees—triangular timbers drifted or through-bolted to the larger timbers—are used to unite the individual pieces into a strong and rigid "backbone." A common source of difficulty in the backbone assembly is the joints where these separate parts are fastened together. Often the "luting" or bedding compound between the pieces leaches out, allowing fresh water and rot spores to enter. With a knife or awl, probe into the knees and adjoining timbers for signs of rot. It may be necessary to remove the rotted sections and replace them or to employ the wood-epoxy saturation technique (West) outlined in the next chapter.

Bolts holding the ballast keel to the keel and keelson often work loose and/or become rusted, and should be inspected annually. After visual inspection, á large socket and breaker-bar should be placed on the nut and an attempt made to get it a turn or so tighter. A heavy-duty railroad-type hex wrench should be used because a standard ratchet handle will surely break. For increased leverage, a two-foot length of pipe may be slipped over the end of the wrench handle.

If the keel bolts revolve when you put the wrench on them, or if you can see a gap between the keel casting and the keel timber, then some of the bolts should be withdrawn for inspection and possible replacement. A good boatyard with a stout marine railway and heavy-duty jacks and tools should be chosen for this work as it is usually beyond the capability of the average boat owner unless he is a very skilled mechanic.

At the same time you check the keel bolts, also check the stem and deadwood bolts. It is not possible to do more than a visual check of the inboard ends and to put a wrench on the nut and test for tightness. If the bolt end is rusted, wire-brush and prime with a rust preventive like Rustoleum. Be sure to keep track of the structural condition of the backbone. If there are checks in the knee running with the grain that also pass through the holes bored for the fastenings, or if the knee seems loose, then it should be replaced. If you are an exemplary craftsman and have the tools, you will probably be able to figure a way to replace knees in an expedient manner. If not, then you should let a competent boatyard handle it.

If the deterioration is not too serious, you can usually make a suitable repair and treat the rotted sections to prevent spread of the decay. When the boat is routinely hauled, open up the cabin sole, remove gear from the vicinity, and let circulation of fresh air flow. With a mixture of warm water, caustic soda, and detergent, scrub the whole area to remove salt, grease, and oil. Flush with fresh water and allow to dry. Cut out any rotted wood that can be removed without causing structural weakness. A sharp chisel and a saw will serve for this purpose. Large checks and cracks may be saturated with epoxy (WEST system, described in the next chapter). When this is finished, the whole area should be doused with Penta, Woodlife, or Cuprinol to destroy and inhibit rot spores. It is not necessary to paint the section—most wood preservatives also serve as a water repellent and will stop grain swelling and checking.

Floor timbers are the triangular pieces of wood that tie together the bottom ends of the frames and the keel; they also form the foundation for the cabin sole. If the bilge is sealed and there is no air flow they frequently deteriorate. While inspecting the hull it is a good practice to wash floor timbers down with caustic soda, rinse, and dry, after which they should be liberally painted with wood preservative. Replacement of loose or structurally unsound floor timbers is a job the owner can do; it is covered in the next chapter.

ON FUNGAL INFECTIONS OF WOOD

Some call it "dry rot," some call it "wet rot," but both are the same thing—a fungal infection caused by an organism that uses the cellulose in the wood for food, eventually destroying its structure. All fungi require moisture to thrive; those that require a great deal produce the so-called wet rot, and those that require less are the so-called dry rot. Since salt inhibits the growth of the organism, fresh water is necessary for proliferation.

Structural defects in the major members of wood boats are caused by this rot, and eventually parts deteriorate and fastenings let go. Since the strength of wood construction depends on having all links in the chain be strong, when one part lets go, all go. Every wooden boat has some degree of rot, and since the spores are airborne they are to some extent present in the lumber from which the boat was built. Rot prevention requires a continuing program of control. The best preventive is a constant flow of fresh air because good ventilation is the enemy of rot; the spores require moisture and ventilation carries away moisture. Also, the fungi are to some extent anaerobic—that is, they thrive only where there is little oxygen—so good air flow cuts rot.

It is also good practice to keep compartmentalization of the hull to a minimum. Doors of lockers and bulkheads should leave space at head and foot or have holes bored top and bottom so that a circulating pattern of air is achieved. When fair days come it should be standard operating procedure to open portholes and insert cowl ventilators into deck vents to air out the interior.

The presence of a ceiling is a very large contributor to rot because of the stagnant air locked in. I always remove a great deal of the ceiling from any boat I buy to permit unrestricted air flow to the frames and inside of the planking. A ceiling beneath berths or in lockers is not necessary and, indeed, I don't even like it in the saloon because I consider the frames and butt blocks and other structural parts pleasing in their detail. In addition, having the frame bays open permits better and quicker damage control in the case of holing—all arguments for an unceiled vessel.

A good program of periodic inspection is the best way to prevent rot. The ship should be carefully inspected every two months. Tools for inspection are a strong flashlight, an awl for probing into the wood, and a hammer for thumping timbers. When rotted wood is struck, the sound has a different quality from that of good wood; wood having rot sounds hollow, dull, or "dead."

Particular attention should be paid to pockets where condensation might gather or where rainwater leaks in. Try to find and stop the leak, then treat the area with fungicide. An excellent practice is to affix panels and other interior joinerwork with through-bolts and/or oval-head screws driven into cupped washers. This will allow easy periodic removal for inspection and fungicidal treatment.

If in the course of normal inspection rot is found, it should be cut away with a sharp chisel, after which the hole must be saturated with a fungicide. If the rot has progressed too far, then the offending piece must be totally removed and replaced. The area where the rotted section butted against good wood must be disinfected with Penta or Cuprinol so that spores are killed.

When rot is in a frame, it is often possible to cut out the bad section and replace it with a new section. This procedure is called "sister framing," and detailed instructions for the technique are found in the next chapter. If rot is only in the end grain and does not seriously affect the structural integrity of the member, an agent which hardens and destroys rot, like the WEST system, will help greatly. But it should not be used where there is extensive deterioration.

Fungicidal Solutions
There are several fungicides and wood preservatives for boats on the market under various names. The most common are pentachorophenol, copper napthanate, and TBTO (tributyl-tin oxide). These chemicals with fungicidal properties are suspended in an oily vehicle; since oil and water are incompatable, they will be absorbed

more readily into dry wood. Copper napthanate solutions, like Cuprinol, are usually green in color, and because of this they are useful for obtaining a visual indication of where treatment has been done. TBTO and pentachlorophenol, unless tinted, are usually clear and are preferred where the wood is to be finished bright. Wood preservative manufacturers usually have full line of products including those for special applications.

Preservatives have a barrier effect on water and act like a paint sealer to reduce shrinking, warping, swelling, and checking of wood. The more saturated the wood, the better the protection. New wood soaked in solution is protected best; new wood with solution liberally brushed on is next best. For old wood, submersion in solution is best, and liberal brushing next. Wood preservatives have strong solvents in their formulas, and although most paints will cover well, paints with a vinyl base should not be used. The oily base will also prevent fiberglass from sticking properly so preservatives should not be used on wood that will later be fiberglassed. In any case, the resin of fiberglass has antirot properties and surface application of wood preservatives is not necessary. Testing done by major fiberglass companies seems to indicate that encasement of sound wood in fiberglass does not promote rot, but on the contrary the resins seem to inhibit it.

MAINTAINING THE BILGE

Beneath the floorboards lies the most important part of the boat insofar as long life is concerned. An "out of sight, out of mind" attitude is common among yacht owners, and for this reason the bilge becomes the source of an enormous amount of trouble. It is my belief that a boat, like an airplane, should have an ongoing monthly inspection program and an annual inspection that is absolutely rigorous. I require that my boats have floor-boards and cabin joinerwork constructed so that they can be disassembled to allow the bilge to be inspected easily.

Floorboards should be of a modular design so they may be taken up with just the simple removal of a few screws. Vertical partitions should be stepped on and fastened to their own footings. Laying the floor first and then erecting partitions and furniture over it is a practice that should be vigorously rejected. If your boat was built in this manner, take the first opportunity to cut along the partitions and cabin sole to make large access hatches. Plenty of clearance should be planed into the boards so that they will not bind when wet and swollen. Synthetic or cocoa matting can be laid to prevent dirt, dust, and lint from falling into the bilge. Oversize pilot holes for fastening the floor boards should be drilled, especially in oak as oak tends to bind severely when swollen. Heavy, nonrusting, flush lifting rings should be fastened to the main boards. Gratings should be fitted at both ends of the sole and in the saloon to allow free air circulation within the bilge.

The basic object of bilge care is to keep the bays clean and free from bacteria. A strong solution of trisodium phosphate—Soilax with detergent, or Clorox and hot water with detergent—should be used to keep the bays free from oil, dirt, and grease. Once a month, scrubbing with a strong solution should be part of routine. A patent bilge cleaner which is just poured into the bilge, permitted to roll about as the boat rolls, and is then pumped out may be used regularly. Once or twice a year after scrubbing and drying of the bilge, the wood should be treated with a fungicide. Take care to work the solution well up into dark corners and into the junction of the frames and the planking. Iron in the bilge should be wire-brushed and painted with Rustoleum or other metal primer and sealer.

Inside Ballast

Many boats have been designed with their ballast, totally
or in part, meant to be carried in the bilge. Such ballast
was lead pigs, iron pigs, or concrete with iron waste or
boiler punchings mixed into the slurry. Ballast lying in
the bilge can create a great deal of dirt and filth as lint
and dust collects. Also, grease and oil adhere to the pigs
and the flow of clean salt water through the bays is ob-
structed. In my opinion the worst offender and rot
breeder is poured concrete ballast. Concrete ballast
traps moisture, prevents free circulation of air, and cannot be easily removed for cleaning of the bilge beneath.

Designers specified this ballast in the past because it
was cheap and because pouring kept the weight down
low in the vessel. Being concrete slurry, it conformed to
the bilge and could not shift in a seaway. But it was
always known that rot proliferated under concrete ballast and for this reason space between the planking and
the ballast was sealed with hot pitch, marine glue, or a
thin grout of Portland cement. It was believed that without a tight bond between ballast and planking, pockets
of water and dirt would form a culture medium for rot.
On the other hand designers also knew that more suitable ballast was available. For the expensive yachts of the
day, lead pigs and iron pigs were preferred over poured
ballast. Pigs could be removed and cleaned and the condition of the bilge ascertained.

With a modern understanding of small-boat maintenance, as I see it—utilizing practices standard in the
aircraft industry—an ongoing maintenance program requires that ballast must be removable so that access to
the vessel's frame is possible. Concrete ballast in older
vessels was economically practical because men lived
aboard these ships and maintained them. There was
plenty of skilled labor available, and if rot developed the
ship could be opened up, bad sections removed, and the

sections rebuilt at little cost. If necessary, sails, spars, ironwork, and machinery could be saved and the whole vessel replaced for a modest investment. Today that is impossible: even if skilled shipbuilders able to frame and plank a hull in the old manner were available in sufficient numbers—which they are not—the cost would be prohibitive. It is the labor which eats the lion's share of money, and materials are next. So every effort should be made to preserve a good old boat.

Lead in rectangular pigs is the preferred ballast for inside trimming. It should be recast to fit between the bays if it is in octagonal shape as it comes from the foundry. Iron pigs should be wire-brushed or sand-blasted, then painted or dipped in epoxy paint to seal out air and water. When locating lead or iron pigs, place them on battens to permit bilge water to flow and to keep from chafing the planking. Sturdy battens should be screwed over the ballast to prevent movement in a seaway. Cement and boiler punchings should be used as ballast only if cost is a primary factor and if it is cast in small pieces with lifting rings so that it may be removed easily for bilge inspection and cleaning.

Limber Holes
Channels for draining the frame bays are called limber holes. They are meant to permit the water in the bilge to drain to a sump at the lowest point, where the pump intake is located. To prevent the accumulation of dirt and places where rot can develop, limber holes must be kept clear and free of debris. It is difficult to keep the drain holes open because hair, lint, dirt, and sand constantly fall into the bilge. Some builders string a brass or bronze chain through the holes with the idea that a pull on the chain will clear the holes. This is not really effective. The only practical solution is to keep the bilge clean by regular washing and by working in the bilge regularly

with a flashlight, sponges, spoons, putty knives, and your fingers to remove junk from the frame bays. Water that comes aboard must drain to the sump quickly, and if it doesn't, something is plugging the limbers. The more time you spend in the bilge, the safer and more wholesome your vessel will be.

Floor Timbers

Floor timbers are the triangular pieces of wood used to join the lower ends of the frames and to fasten the futtocks to the keel. Floor timbers should be washed with trisodium phosphate to remove oil and grease, and the wood checked carefully for rot or splits. If the wood is sound, it should be treated with a preservative. If the structural integrity of the floors is questionable, they should be removed and replaced following the procedures outlined in the next chapter.

Engine Drip Pans

Oil and grease in the bilge prevent the wood from breathing by creating a film that traps moisture. Leaking lubricants from engine oil seals, gearbox, and oil sump are the greatest single offender in this respect. It is good operating procedure to install an engine drip pan beneath the engine. When a new engine is installed this is easy, but much more difficult with an older installation. One way to build a drip pan easily is to work a piece of copper screen under the engine and gearbox, then to fiberglass the screen with saturated resin strips. Brushes with long handles or rags tied to sticks can be utilized to wet out the strips with resin. A pipe nipple and plug may be fitted to the screen at the lowest point so that the pan can be cleaned by flushing. If there is no room for a pipe nipple, leave a low spot as a sump for a portable transfer pump such as used for changing oil. A drip pan in the engine compartment will go a long way toward maintaining a clean and wholesome bilge.

How to Paint the Wood Boat

It is more important with wood than with any other boat-building material that a paint barrier to prevent deterioration from weathering be properly applied. Good painting procedures should be followed and ongoing maintenance should be routine. Once deterioration sets in it can progress rapidly, but with care a wood boat can be made to last indefinitely. The major enemies of wood boats are fresh water, which supports the growth of mold and rot, and drying out, which causes alternate swelling and shrinking, testing the elasticity of the wood to the maximum. The use of paint, preservatives, fungicides, and water repellents will control these enemies of wood.

If you have not already done so, now is a good time to go back and read the chapters on paint systems and on painting the fiberglass boat because many useful hints are contained there that will apply to painting the wood boat as well.

First, all gear should be taken from the boat interior and stored indoors. It will later be gone over carefully when time permits. If there are any small black spots indicating mildew or if the cabin smells musty, the interior should be washed down with a solution made of 1 cup trisodium phosphate (Soilax or Oakite), ½ cup detergent, and 1 cup sodium hypochlorite (Clorox) to one bucket of hot water. When you have finished washing, rinse the area with a light spray from a hose. If mildew is a constant problem, then it is certain that there is no free flow of ventilating air. Try to get more air flow by installing scoop ventilators in the overhead and grille ventilators in closet doors, bulkheads, and beneath furniture to bring air to stagnant pockets. An effective remedy, if the cabin is to be repainted, is to put a mildew-preventive such as Woolsey's Mildoom into the paint. This will inhibit further growth.

A good washing down after the boat is hauled is imperative. Grease, chemical film, and salt must be removed if a good bond is to be made with the new paint. Trisodium phosphate or a patent solution should be used with hot water to scrub the hull clean, followed by a rinsing with a hose and fresh water. The boat should then be allowed to dry thoroughly.

After barnacles and marine organisms are scraped off, the wood beneath should be checked for damage. Fittings that are hard to cut in with a paint brush should be removed. While you are waiting for successive coats to dry or on days of bad weather, you can clean, brush, and paint these fittings indoors.

Preparing the Surface

To a great extent, the lasting quality and success of the paint job on a wooden hull depends on the care taken in preparing the surface. A good sanding with medium-grade paper will be sufficient preparation if the existing paint still has a good bond without alligatoring, wrinkles, blisters, or entrapped moisture pockets. If defects are present, they must be scraped open with a hook or triangular scraper, the moisture allowed to dry, and a primer coat of paint and trowel cement applied. The depression must be made flush with the surrounding surface, then primed again and sanded. New plastic, long-lasting, quick-drying trowel cements are made by many manufacturers. Techniques for their use are in Chapter 5.

Wooding Down

A condition that is called "paint sick" exists when many coats of paint have built up over the years. This condition requires that the hull be brought back to bare wood, after which new priming and finish coats are applied. Do not use a blowtorch to remove built-up paint as the intense heat causes embrittlement of the wood. Instead, use a propane torch with a wide nozzle. Apply the heat only until the paint begins to blister and then lift it off with a wide-bladed putty knife. Keep the torch moving and only do small areas at a time. When liquid or paste remover is used, be sure to wipe with a solvent and wash with a strong Soilax solution and rinse. If this is not done, the oily base of the removers will cause bonding difficulties with the new paint.

A Note on Sanding

For fine work it is best to hand sand. If the amount of surface to be covered is considerable, an oscillating sander may be used. Try to get a "straight-line" rather than an orbital one because the orbital sander leaves small circles on the surface. Belt sanders should only be used for rough work as it is practically impossible to control a belt sander carefully enough to avoid gouging the surface. For removing built-up bottom paint, a coarse disc on an electric drill or a heavy-duty disc sander is useful. Because the abraded material is highly toxic, a good respirator must always be used. Running your hand over the surface will reveal any unfairness which the eye did not catch but which will appear through gloss paint.

Choosing the Paint System

If synthetic paints are used on the wooden boat, care should be taken to follow the manufacturer's directions to the letter for thinning, priming, and application. One of the epoxy formulations should be considered if you have been having paint trouble because their chemical and adhesion characteristics are superior. The choice of antifouling will depend on the nature of your home waters and the organisms found there. The best practice is to survey your fellow yachtsmen to find what works for them. Experience here is the best criterion. Though surface preparation takes longer, painting of wood boats is easier than with most others. Again, reread the sections in this book on paint systems before beginning work.

9. How to Make Repairs and Modifications to Wood Boats

Many boat owners have had some training in carpentry and some are skillful in the use of tools. For the benefit of yachtsmen, the information in this chapter will outline procedures for completing the most commonly needed repairs to the wood boat.

But if you lack such skills it might be useful to attend a night course in woodworking at your local high school. If you can use a saw, sharpen a plane blade, or prebore and drive a screw properly, then except for major structural repairs, you should be able to do a considerable amount of repair work yourself.

It is impossible to cover all the repairs that may be encountered by the boat owner, so what I will do is explain techniques for repairing the most common structural deficiencies that you are likely to find in buying or operating a used wood boat. Here are the modern methods for putting in a new floor timber, replacing a section of planking, and repairing a broken frame. I will show you the measuring and templating tricks of the professionals, and everything you need to know to build in any cabin furniture you desire. In doing these tasks, you will gain satisfaction and a skill that will afford you pleasure and pride all your life.

MAKING THE NEW PIECE FIT: TECHNIQUES OF
TEMPLATING, SCRIBING, SPILING, AND MEASURING

Professional boatbuilders have several methods for fitting new woodwork to compound curves in an easy, accurate way. Some of these methods I will now discuss before you put them into practice.

It is easier to obtain true reference lines if the hull is first leveled in a fore-and-aft and thwartships attitude. If the boat is still in the water, provided she is properly trimmed she will automatically level herself in all directions. If in the stocks ashore, she should be leveled before proceeding. A plumb bob should be hung from the exact center of cabin top beams both forward and aft of the center of gravity—which is more or less in the middle of the boat measured from the stemhead and the transom. The boat should then be chocked and wedged until the point of the plumb bob centers exactly on a line marking the keel centerline. The centerline on the beam and the centerline of the keel, your major references, are obtained by measuring an equal distance from the outboard edges of both members.

To level fore-and-aft, good-quality spirit levels are held against vertical bulkheads also fore and aft of the center of gravity. The reading should be taken simultaneously, and it is useful to have two persons taking the readings while the bow or stern is raised or lowered by the use of chocks and wedges until the bubble in the spirit shows level. One must be careful that there is no wracking or twisting of the hull along the longitudinal or horizontal axis. The best way to discover such twisting is to sight along the cabin trunk or the toe-rail at the sheer.

The eye is the best judge for this purpose. Do not be afraid to make adjustments from this information, for the eye is an excellent tool. The reason for using levels in front of and behind the center of gravity is that with a long-ended vessel or a fin-keel vessel with considerable overhang, it would be possible to have an indication of level at a midships bulkhead while there could exist a droop at the extreme ends which would be definitely out of level. Simultaneous leveling at several places fore and aft of the center of gravity prevents this from happening.

Scribing to a Curve

A technique which you will resort to constantly is called "scribing." It is extremely useful if properly done. The most common error in scribing is committed by not holding the plane of the compass perpendicular to either the vertical or the horizontal plane, depending on the nature of the line you must draw. The tendency is to keep the axis of the compass (a line drawn between the pencil and the sharp leg) perpendicular to the *arc of the curve* to be reproduced. This will not work, as you can see from the Figure 9. The reason becomes clear if you scribe two semicircles, one inside the other. The second semicircle has to be of smaller radius and therefore cannot fit exactly into the first. A useful rule of thumb to scribe a line for a piece that has its major direction up and down—for example, to fit against the outboard side of a bulkhead where it bears against the planking—is to hold the plane of the compass parallel to the waterline and draw it straight up and down. On the other hand, if the line required is primarily horizontal—as for fitting a piece against the cabin top or a deck beam—then keep the two points of the compass perpendicular to the thwartships waterline. Take care as you draw the compass along that the axis does not inadvertently change.

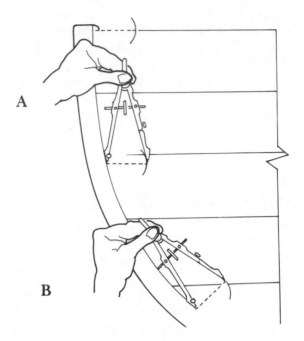

Figure 9. Scribing New Work to Fit a Curve. A. Correct. *Keep the compass horizontal, or at right angles to an imaginary vertical line, when scribing for planking and bulkheads.* **B.** Incorrect. *If the compass is held as a radius to the curve, or perpendicular to the arc, then the cut piece will be too small.*

Fitting by Back Measuring

Back measuring is a useful technique for fitting relatively short sections to irregular configurations. A line 3 or 4 feet long is about all that can be projected at a time with this method unless you are extremely deft and experienced. The principles of back measuring are easily understood by referring to Figure 10, but are somewhat difficult to convey with words. A piece of thin wood or thick cardboard is roughly cut to the curve to be fitted. The template is then tacked against the part to be fitted. If there is any curve to the section, a pencil compass is used to scribe. The compass should be opened to span the maximum width between the section and the template. Next, a carpenter's rule is held against projecting members and their angle of intercept with the template is marked. Depths, widths, and angles are measured and marked on the template—a look at Figure 10 will show how this is done. A cardboard template may be cut with scissors to the line and tried against the section for fit.

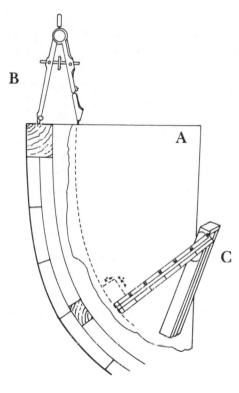

Figure 10. Fitting by Back Measuring. A. *Rough out a template to butt against the section to be fitted.* **B.** *Scribe the curves on the template with a compass.* **C.** *Mark the protrusions on the template by measuring back from the scribed curves. Once the template is complete, lay it on the new stock and reverse the marking process.*

If it is accurate it may now be laid on the new stock and traced in outline. If the template is too stiff to cut, then it may be laid on the new stock and the outline marked by back measuring in reverse. This process is not as complicated as it sounds and a few practice attempts will make it easy.

Template Fitting

Whenever difficult shapes must be fitted, the best practice is to make an exact template, thereby guaranteeing perfect fit. For small sections, patterns may be cut from shirt cardboards which are stapled or taped together to form a pattern large enough to cover the repair. For bulkheads or other large sections, a straight-grained, clear 2 × 4 may be cut into thin laths on a table saw with a ripping blade attached. The laths are then tacked together with small brads to form a lattice outline of the required shape. The lattice can be combined with shirt-cardboards stapled to the edges of the template for more accurate delineation of difficult shapes (see Figure 11). Measurements for transferring the shape to new stock are obtained by back measuring, scribing, and cut-and-fit. To transfer the outline to the new stock, the template is laid down and lightly tacked with brads so that it does not move, and the outline is traced.

Spiling to Fit

An extremely handy method of fitting a long repair section such as a plank replacement is called "spiling." There are several variant methods of spiling. In use, a long, thin batten which fits handily into the space to be fitted is cut and tacked against the frames to hold it in place. Sufficient space is allowed so that there is no binding, and care must be taken so that the spiling batten does not take an edge set. If any set is taken, the batten

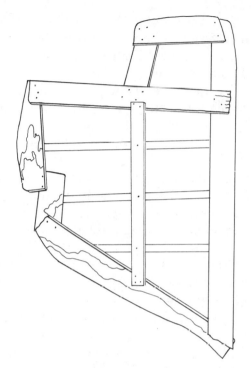

Figure 11. Making a Composite Template for Large Panels. *When large panels (like plywood bulkheads) must be fitted, rough-cut shirt cardboards or thin wood template stock to fit close to the edges of the bulkhead. Using small brads, nail together a latticework to hold the template together while it is removed and laid on the new stock for tracing. Curved and difficult sections may be outlined by back measuring and scribing.*

will spring out of shape when it is removed to transfer spiling marks. A piece of ⅛ - or ¼ -inch plywood makes good spiling battens. To spile, the batten is just bent in a fair, sweeping curve that it will easily keep and is lightly tacked with fine brads. Now, a compass with pencil is opened to a span which is slightly larger than the greatest distance between the inner edge of the planking and the spiling batten. The compass is swung in short sections of arc onto the spiling batten. The more the plank varies from a straight line, the closer together the arcs should be swept in (see Figure 12A). The point of the compass is placed against the inner edge of the plank because this is the edge of the plank that must fit. If the point were placed on the outer edge of the plank, the bevel planed on the plank to accommodate caulking would make the plank outsized and it would not fit. This is really hair-splitting because such tolerances are seldom achieved. When cutting to the line with new stock, most craftsmen cut lightly outside the line as a precaution against ruining an expensive piece of lumber. A dressing with a plane is generally necessary for a perfect fit.

The next step is to transfer the outline of the piece to the new lumber stock. The spiling batten is laid on the stock and lightly tacked to hold it in place. The batten should be moved about to avoid knots or checks and so that there is minimum wastage. One point of the dividers is placed at the top of the arcs on the batten and new arcs are swept onto the stock (see Figure 12B). The spiling board then is removed, a flexible batten is tacked tangent to the arcs on the stock, and the outline is drawn in with a carpenter's pencil. This is the shape to which the plank must be sawn on a band saw or, if the curves are not too great, on a table saw.

Another tool for spiling, which utilizes not a compass but a "spiling block," is shown in Figure 13. This method works more easily than the traditional compass method and is equally accurate.

REFITTING FLOORS

It is often the case that floor timbers become soft or badly checked and no longer serve their function, which is to tie together the frame ends and the keel. In most

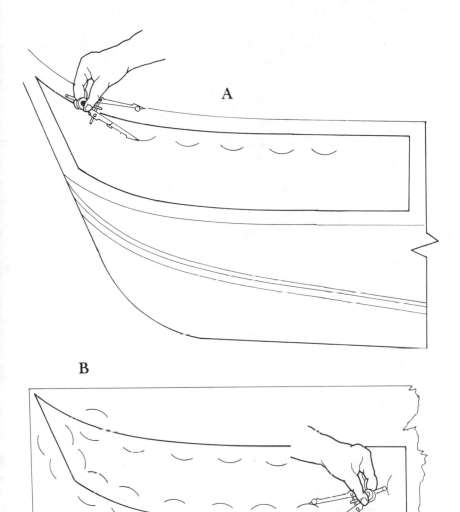

Figure 12. Spiling to Fit. A. *Bend and fasten with brads a thin spiling batten in the space where the new plank is to be fitted. Open a marking compass and place the sharp point against the inside edge of the plank. Sweep in arcs at regular intervals; where the curve of the plank is greatest the arcs should be close together.* **B.** *To transfer the outline to the new stock, tack the spiling batten to the new plank material and reverse the process without changing the opening of the compass. Draw a line tangent to the transferred arcs to be used to guide cutting out the replacement plank on the band saw.*

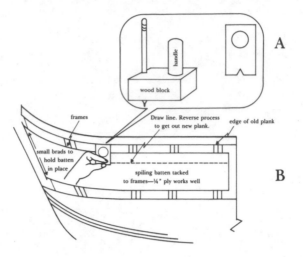

Figure 13. Using a Spiling Block. A. *A "spiling block" which is easier to use than dividers may be made from a small block of wood. A dowel handle may be drilled in and a notch is cut for seating a pencil.* **B.** *To use the spiling block instead of a pair of dividers to get out a new plank, slide the block along the edge of the old plank and trace the outline on the flat spiling batten tacked to the frames. To get the outline of a new plank, tack the spiling batten on the new stock and just reverse the process.*

cases it will prove easiest to remove the old floor timber in pieces. A few saw cuts down the timber, a ripping hammer, a narrow-bladed lathing hatchet, and an all-metal flooring chisel are the best tools for breaking out the old floor. Floors are fastened to the keel and to the frame ends by several different kinds of fastenings. One such fastening is drift pins, which are just huge nails driven at an angle into the keel. The blows from the hammer form a head on the end of the pin like a rivet head. It is impossible to draw out well-driven drift pins, so the floors must be split out and the drifts cut off flush with the keel, after which they should be primed and painted with epoxy.

The small bolts holding the floor timbers to the ends

of the frames are removed by cutting with a hacksaw and punching out with a machinist's punch (see Figure 14). Do not try to remove them by knocking the nuts and short ends off with a cold chisel. The force of the blows will distort and split the frame ends. This is undesirable.

Using the template method of reproduction, new patterns are made for the floors and a small adjustable bevel is used to take off the outboard bevels. The procedure for doing this is illustrated in Figure 15.

After the new floors are made, they are fastened to the keel with drifts made from silicon-bronze or Monel rod (see Fig. 14C). I prefer Monel as it is easier to drive without bending or distortion. The tip of the rod is formed into a rough point by pounding it with a hammer on an anvil. A tight-fitting washer called a "clench ring" is dropped over the top of the rod. The blows of the driving sledge will upset the rod sufficiently to form a good head which will fit down into the recess of the washer. The pins are driven into prebored, tight-fitting holes after lubricating the shafts with soft brown soap. Be careful when boring not to strike the old drift pins which were cut off and left in the keel timber.

If the wood at the frame ends is sound and the bolts into the frames have been cleanly punched out, the old holes may be reused by reaming them slightly with an electric drill and then employing an oversize bolt. If the holes are in poor condition, they should be plugged with dowels and epoxy glue. New holes should then be bored to fasten the frames to the floors.

Some floors will have been picked by the designer to carry the bolts holding the ballast to the keel. Ballast bolts are driven from the outside of the hull up through the ballast keel, through the keel timber, and up through the floor, where they terminate in a large washer and nut. By heating and dousing with Liquid Wrench, it is often

A

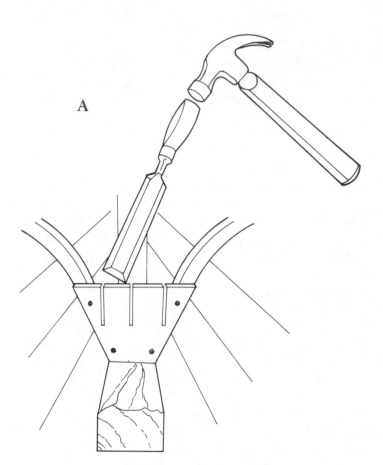

Figure 14. Removing and Replacing Bad Floor Timbers. A. *Remove the old floors by splitting them out with a thin lathing hatchet or a large chisel. Saw cuts down the floors will facilitate removal.* **B.** *Remove the bolts holding the floors to the frame ends by cutting off the nuts with a hacksaw. Drive out the old bolts with a heavy hammer and a machinist's punch.* **C.** *Floors that do not house a ballast bolt may be simply replaced and fastened by driving new drift pins of Monel, stainless-steel, or bronze rod. A coating of brown soap will lubricate the drift pins and help in driving them.* **D.** *Floors in the way of ballast bolts may be made in two pieces and glued together with Chem-Tech T-88 or WEST SYSTEM® brand epoxy. If the ballast-bolt nut will not turn off, epoxy-coated wedge washers may be made and driven to bring the floor tight to the keel.*

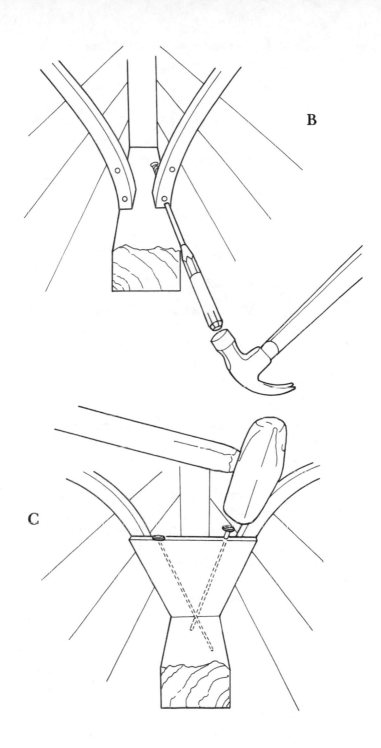

B

C

D

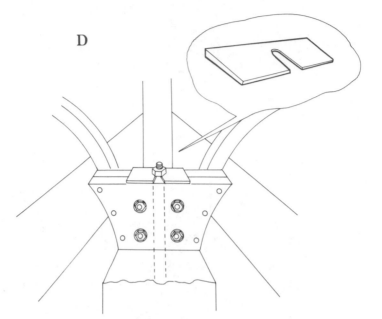

possible to turn off ballast bolt nuts. Be extremely careful, however, to avoid damaging the threads. If the ballast bolt nuts come off handily, you can make a new floor,
bore it for the bolt, grease the hole, wrap cotton wicking
soaked in paint around the bolt, and drive the new floor
on with a wooden mallet.

It will generally be the case that the bolt you are working on will only be carrying a part of the weight of the
ballast keel and will probably be so siezed that it will not
drop. However, it is a good idea to shore up the ballast
keel so there is no sag after the nut is removed.

If the ballast bolt nuts do not come off after a reasonable series of efforts, such as heating and saturation with
a thread solvent, then do not risk ruining the ballast bolt.
Instead, the new floor may be put back around the ballast
bolt in two pieces, which is preferable to replacing a

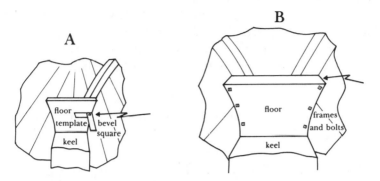

Taking off bevels for new floor.

Cut resultant angle on edges of floor timber with bandsaw set to same angle. Fasten new floor to frame ends with stainless stove bolts.

Figure 15. Using a Bevel to Take Off the Outboard Bevels. A. *Measure the angle between planking and frame with a small adjustable bevel square. If bevel square is not available, make one from two pieces of broken hacksaw blade with bolt and wing nut through blade end-holes.* **B.** *Transfer the angle to the side of the new floor timber, mark, and saw on bandsaw to achieve fit as in Figure 15B.*

ballast bolt (see Figure 14D). The best way to do this is to take off outline and bevels and get out the new floor in one piece. Mark and bore the hole for the ballast bolt, and then rip the new floor carefully down the thwartships centerline on a bandsaw having a thin blade. The extra material taken off by the saw kerf will usually prove sufficient to allow for a generous application of glue. Chem-Tech T-88 or WEST SYSTEM[R] brand epoxy should be used on faying surfaces. Next, carriage bolts should be driven through the floors and the frame ends, and the nuts brought up just tight enough to force the glue out at the glueline. Bring each nut up a few turns at a time as one does with wheel nuts on a car so you do not split the new floor. Frame end fastenings and the ballast bolt will be sufficient to securely fasten floors that come in the way of ballast bolts. No drifts will be necessary.

To bring a holding strain on the new assembly, a rectangular washer is made and a shallow bevel is ground in. This may be supplemented with a duplicate mate which is driven from the opposite side. To use, the washers are dunked in catalyzed epoxy and then driven under the ballast bolt nut to bring it tight to the new floor timber.

WEST SYSTEM® BRAND PRODUCTS—AN IMPORTANT DEVELOPMENT

As we proceed in this chapter I will outline methods for completing several very useful repairs and modifications for wooden boats. Replacing a broken or rotted frame, replacing a section of damaged planking, and building in new cabin joinerwork competently are extremely useful skills. Since my first book on boat maintenance, an extremely versatile method of working with wood has been developed that has caused me to change my thinking slightly about the best way to approach certain jobs.

The techniques I refer to arise from the procedures and products developed by Gougeon Brothers in Bay City, Michigan. In brief, the WEST SYSTEM® considers wood as a matrix material much like fiberglass (but in some ways better), which when saturated with various epoxy mixtures exhibits a synergistic effect. WEST SYSTEM® epoxy may be used in many boatbuilding applications but it is in *laminating* that I find it to excel.

Boatbuilding wood in suitable scantlings is becoming increasing difficult to obtain. A superior adhesive which prevents water absorption, delamination, and distortion from humidity seems to have admirably overcome objections to wood construction. Also, the use of lamination techniques has greatly solved the problem of shortage or nonexistence of men with the extremely hard-learned skills necessary to fabricate the complex, compound shapes found in boats. It is a deft art, indeed, which can take a 4-inch-thick oak slab, loft it to the shape of a sawn frame, cut, dress, fit, and fasten it, all within master shipwright tolerances. That measure of experience and craft is gone, as are the materials, and new techniques must make up for the lack.

To replace a broken frame or to sister-frame as outlined in the following section, WEST SYSTEM® epoxy is by far the preferred and easiest method of repair. Resorcinol glues, although they still have their place in boat work, must take second place to the epoxy-saturation technique for quality of bond. And in the fabrication of interior joinerwork, lamination, and filleting fastening of partitions and bulkheads, it is highly recommended.

Also highly recommended is the excellent manual published by Gougeon Brothers detailing their methodology and their products (the address of this company is listed on page 180 of this book). I will speak of WEST SYSTEM® products constantly in the forthcoming material but only in general terms. For details of construction and characteristics of resins, the reader is urged to purchase the small WEST SYSTEM® manual, which sells for only $2 dollars—it is well worth the investment.

SISTER-FRAMING THE WOOD BOAT

If the planking is sound but the frames of your boat are rotted or broken, it is desirable to replace or "sister-frame" next to the old futtock to restore the structural integrity of the hull. In order to provide room to work, the ceiling should be removed in the way of the damaged frames. Cabin joinerwork that interferes with access will also have to be dismantled temporarily.

To reinforce bad frames, either sawn frames or steam-bent frames can be utilized. Refitting sawn frames, however, requires a great deal of skill to take off the changing bevels from the planking and frame angles, and then to reproduce the changing bevels continuously as you cut the frames on the band saw.

Steaming is somewhat easier, but a steam box must be made and suitable oak bending stock must be obtained. A helper is needed to pass the hot frames and to assist with the fastening before the frames cool. A much better and easier method of sister-framing is to laminate the frames right in place. This is done by getting out a series of thin strips of ½ inch or less in thickness and as wide as needed. They are then bent to the required curve and glued together in a kind of "sandwich." Until the development of resorcinol glues this method of construction was subject to delamination and could only be used in low-humidity environments. Now, epoxy glue formulations, and especially WEST SYSTEM® epoxy, not only make for a lamination which does not come apart, but it is no longer necessary to dress the faying surfaces to absolute smoothness in order to guarantee a nonfailing bond. In addition, the epoxy mixtures are not pressure-critical and the catalyzed resin flows into the space between the surfaces to fill up voids. The excess resin is squeezed out by the clamps or fastenings and then wiped off; bonding is not dependent on a super-quality joint. A further advantage of WEST SYSTEM® laminating is that the resins seem to exhibit a fungicidal effect which produces a long-lasting sister frame resistant to rot and as strong or stronger than a steam-bent frame of the same wood.

When choosing lumber for laminating frames, pick a strong, supple variety. The traditional best is white oak or elm, which are, however, now difficult to obtain. Douglas fir marine-grade plywood will make suitable frames provided the curve is not so great that compression strain on the surface ruptures the plies.

The width of the new frame should be at least equal to the old but may be made wider for additional strength.

Pick pieces free of checks and knots. A belt sander should be used to remove saw kerf marks or planer marks from the stock before application of resin.

The method of laminating is more easily represented in Figure 16 than in words. When the sections to be repaired are gentle in curve or short in length, the layers may be glued and screwed as you go along. If the sections are long, or if there is much curvature, then the clamp bolts shown in Figure 16 will be necessary. Only sufficient bolts to bring in the curvature (or the number of fastenings normally used in such a frame) should be employed or the frame will be weakened. One can use shores inside to keep tension on shallow curves. If temporary clamp bolts are made from ¼-inch carriage bolts, this will prevent the outer blocks from turning. An assistant to hold a wrench on the outside of the hull is not necessary.

The trickiest part of the job will be to drill the holes in each strip so they accurately line up with the bolts. This can be more easily done by removing the wing nuts and blocks after the prior glue line has set and forcing the new strip in so it lies alongside the bolts. Location of the holes for the bolts can be marked on each strip by squaring out from the centerline of the bolt. Be careful to mark the center of the strip so edges of the new frame fall flush and not all out of line. As each new laminate hardens, it will remain in place and wing nuts may be removed and a new strip forced on.

When the new frame has totally cured, the bolts that were used as clamps should be removed and replaced with permanent ¼-inch flat-head stove bolts. Elastomeric sealant or epoxy glue should be smeared around the shaft of the new bolt, and washers should be placed over the bolt on the inside of the frames only (see Figure 16E). This will prevent leakage into the hull through the

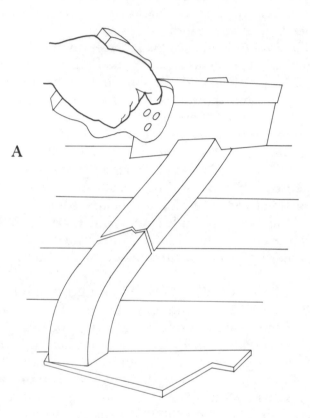

A

Figure 16. How to Sister-Frame a Boat. A. *Using a sharp carpenter's crosscut saw, cut away the broken or rotted section of the frame.* **B.** *Once the old frame section is removed, plug the holes left in the planks by the old fastenings with dowels set in catalyzed epoxy. Bend a batten the same width as the new frame and mark off the outlines of the sister frame.* **C.** *Force the first laminate strip against the inside of the hull and then drill ¼" diameter holes through both the laminate and the hull planking. Take care to avoid seams when drilling. Holes for bolts are only needed where the curve is greatest.* **D.** *When used with ¼" bolts or threaded rods, large wing nuts and wood blocks serve as clamps to hold the laminate in place. Brush Chem-Tech T-88 glue or WEST SYSTEM® brand epoxy on the outboard face of the laminate before putting the laminate in place and tightening the wing nuts.* **E.** *When the lamination has set, remove the wing nuts, prepare the next layer of laminate, brush it with the glue or epoxy, fit if over the last layer, and replace and tighten the wing nuts to clamp it in place.* **F.** *When the final lamination has cured, remove the wing nuts and knock out the temporary clamps, replacing them with ¼" bronze bolts with nuts and washers. Finally, plug and seal the outboard fastener holes.*

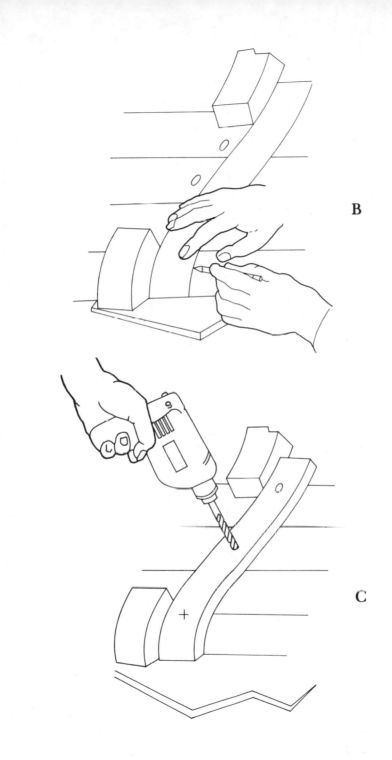

B

C

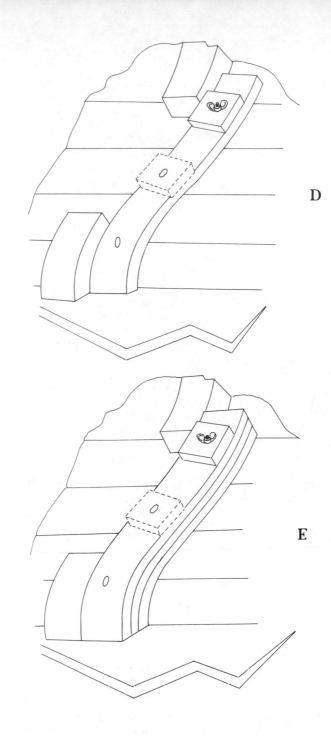

D

E

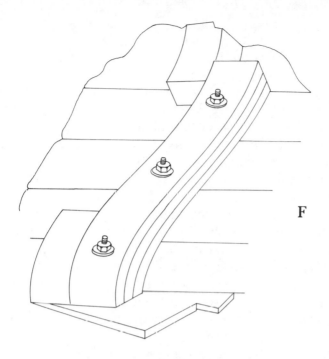

F

frame hole. Do not be tempted to use brass bolts, for they will corrode and wring off; you will have a leaking boat and all your work will be for nothing. Stick with Monel or silicon-bronze.

This lamination technique may also be used for replacement of cabin top overhead beams or for building a foundation against which to fasten a new bulkhead or door. Generally, bolt clamps will not be necessary in such applications as it is easier to utilize shores and wedges in this space.

A week after the laminations have cured, it is good practice to go back and take another turn or two on the nuts to bring them up tight. The surplus inside the hull should be cut off with a hacksaw. A ball-peen hammer may be used to rivet over the bolt end to prevent the nut from loosening. The size of the bolts utilized should be proportional to the width of the frame—¼-inch bolts are generally suitable for a small boat.

HOW TO REPLACE A PLANK

A very common repair which must be made on a wood boat will involve the replacement of a section of planking that has become severely abraded from scraping against docks or split and cracked from impact. It is not difficult to replace planking properly, but it requires honest workmanship.

To begin, look over the planking carefully and determine how much must be removed to make a sound hull. Generally, two different types of planking repair will be encountered. The first is where the section of planking to be replaced butts into the rabbet at bow or stern. This requires that only one cut will have to be made to free the plank. The other repair is when the damaged section is at or near a midships section and requires two cuts to free the damaged section.

The same techniques are employed for the repair of both kinds of damage, but a repair to the center of a plank is somewhat less critical because you do not have to take into account the need to remove planking without damaging the rabbet. When the hood end of the planking lies in the rabbet, it requires considerable care to remove it in a manner that does not break out chunks of the stem within the rabbet. If damage is done to the rabbet, refastening the new plank is difficult. The best procedure is to cut the plank just aft of the bow rabbet or just forward of the stern rabbet. The piece should be removed by splitting a little at a time with a sharp chisel and the remaining screws can then be turned out with a pair of large vise-grips.

When repairing the planking of your boat, you must take care that the new sections are not too short. The reason for this is that trees have a "set" grown into the fibers, which are a factor in the nature of the lumber that is cut from the trunk. The cut plank tends to resist pressures which would alter it from this natural shape. When such a plank is bent around the frames of a boat, the plank is required to assume a new shape contrary to the natural set. In order for this new shape to remain, sufficient fastenings must be driven so that constant pressure is exerted on the plank. After a time the fibers will stretch and compress and will no longer have a tendency to spring out, but will conform to the new shape.

Many strakes of short-length planking, especially when the butts fall close together, seriously weaken a hull. No plank should be replaced that is less than three or four frames in length, and the butts should be planned so that there are at least four strakes of planking between butts. A frequent violation of this good practice occurs when a yard replaces a section of rotted stem. In order to gain access to the stem they will sometimes cut bow planking back a few feet, replace the stem, and then replace the short lengths of plank. This should never be done, for the bow will work, the fastenings will chew into the wood, and the bow seams will open. Do not permit anyone to make this kind of repair, even if it means replanking half the hull from sheer to waterline.

Before new work can begin, the old plank must be removed and the opening cleaned up so that measurements may be taken. The section of plank to be cut should be squared to the seam with a try-square. A hole for a saber or keyhole saw is drilled and the plank cut down the line, taking care not to damage the edge of the good planking. An alternative to square-cutting the edge is to bevel it so that scarfed planking using the WEST SYSTEM® can be utilized. This will be covered in the material on page 186.

Now, chisel around the fastenings with a very sharp wood chisel. A circle-cutting saw may also be chucked in a variable-speed electric drill for this purpose. The saw is held perpendicular to the surface of the planking and a cut is made that does not quite come through the inner surface of the planking. To facilitate removal of the plank, more saber-saw cuts can be made at 1-foot intervals. A hammer with ripping claws, several sharp all-steel electrician's chisels, and a small crowbar are the tools for splitting out the old plank. Be careful when pulling off the old plank that the caulking and sealer in the seam does not adhere to and rupture the edge of the good plank above and below. Proceed slowly and watch the effect of your work as you go along.

If at all possible, old fastenings should be removed and the holes filled with dowels dipped in epoxy glue. Ones that are absolutely impossible to remove should be cut off, but care must be taken not to hit them when boring for the new fastenings.

Check the condition of the framing now while the interior of the hull is accessible. If the framing is not in good condition in some areas, short sections of sister framing may be required so the new fastenings will hold securely. While the frames are open to sight, wood preservative may be brushed liberally on everything you can reach.

The new plank is now gotten out from clear, knot-free stock. Wherever possible replace the plank with the same kind of wood as the original planking. This is not always possible but the attempt should be made. At least try to find a wood with the same hardness and bending characteristics.

You have already gotten the shape of the plank from the spiling you made (as outlined on page 156). Now the plank is cut. The best tool for this is a small power hand saw with an extremely sharp ripping blade. Have several new blades handy for this operation. In violation of all the safety rules, the saw guard must be removed from the saw or wired up so that you can watch the kerf. Be very careful to hold the saw firmly, drape the electric cord over your shoulder so it stays away from the blade, and stand to one side, not directly behind the saw. Have a helper drop wooden wedges into the kerf several feet behind the blade to keep the off-cut strip from binding the saw. You should also have a helper hold up the long waste cut as you near the end of the plank. Be sure the new stock is supported well on sawhorses or a proper cutting bench. The end that fits into the rabbet can be cut with a heavy-duty saber saw. After the plank is cut to shape, it should be dressed with a jack plane set to a fine cut. Plane the plank until it fits perfectly on its inside edge, top and bottom with the existing planks. The outer edge of the new plank must now be planed to a slight bevel for about a third of its width to make a seam to receive the cotton caulking. If the plank rests against a portion of the hull having a great deal of round, as in a midships section at the turn of the bilge, for example, you will have to plane-in a hollow with a scrub plane so that the plank rests fairly against the frame. It will also be necessary to plane the outer surface of the plank so it conforms with the old planking. Be certain, therefore, that the thickness of the new plank is sufficient to allow for this extra dressing.

When the plank has been tried and fitted it is time to get out the butt blocks. These will be large enough to overlap half a plank width above and beneath the repair. The outboard face of the butt block should be rounded to fit fairly against the plank, and there should be room for at least five fastenings on each side of the butt. A luting material such as Thiokol is painted or smeared on the butt block before fastening the plank.

The next step is to drive a few fastenings and to spring-in the plank to bear on the frames. It will require some accessories and some care to do this. If the plank will not spring in without danger of breaking, a steam box may be made by cutting the end out of an old hot-water boiler and building a fire under it. The plank can be boiled first and if it still does not flex in, it may be steamed. While the plank is still wet, a propane torch with a wide nozzle can be utilized by a helper to keep the plank hot while the fastenings are being driven. This keeps the plank supple, but be sure to keep the torch moving so the wood is not embrittled.

C-clamps can be used to bring in planks for fastening when several planks are being replaced, but when you come to the last or "shutter" strake, it will require some ingenuity and special techniques for springing-in the shutter to the frame tight enough for fastening. Shores and wedges to the roof beams and walls can be utilized, and uprights can be buried into the ground to provide bearing for wedges. Also, an old auto jack can be fastened to a 4 × 4 to make a compression tool for springing-in planking. Rent-a-Tool companies often have screw-end lolly columns for use in house construction that are very useful for forcing in the shutter strake. Your ingenuity, too, will be helpful in solving this shutter problem.

Silicon-bronze screws or Anchorfast Monel nails are the preferred fastening into the frames. Butt blocks should be used inside the hull. Before final fastening, the butt block and the rabbet should be luted well with elastomeric sealant. Some builders lute the whole rabbet and then screw in the planks, but I prefer to lute the plank hood end and then screw the plank in, as I feel this makes for cleaner working.

All fastenings into the stem and frames should be prebored. Patent boring tools which bore for threads, shank head, and countersink, as I have already pointed out, are available from marine supply or good hardware stores. Professionals usually drive screws with a heavy-duty Yankee ratchet screwdriver first, and then use a ratchet brace with a screwdriver bit to send the screw home and bring in the plank. If you drive a bad fastening, remove it, plug the hole with a dowel dipped in epoxy, and rebore for another one alongside it. Brown soap scraped over the screw threads makes driving easier. When the plank is finally in place it may be caulked with elastomeric as depicted in Chapter 8, page 25ff. It is then planed, sanded smooth, and given a primer of thinned paint.

In lieu of fastening planks with butt blocks at the end, a bevel can be planed on both ends of the new plank and on the ends of the old plank. The bevels are matched and coated with WEST SYSTEM® epoxy and drawn in with clamps. The epoxy is sufficient to bond the ends, but a few flat-head stove bolts may be used as a safety factor. The bevel for this type of construction, which does not require butt blocks, must be made on a ratio of about 8 to 1 so there is sufficient bonding area for a good joint.

When caulking the seams after a new plank has been installed, it is desirable to caulk lightly at first until the characteristics of the new plank in the water environment are known. Rely on the elastomeric for the major sealing. It should prove sufficient for good watertightness.

THE CURE FOR LEAKING DECKS

No one can sleep at night with the constant drip of cold water splatting onto his berth. Yet finding and fixing deck leaks is one of the most frustrating and annoying things the boat owner has to do. It is possible to end deck leaks forever, however, by laminating a new deck over the old.

The way to do this is to remove the old canvas, all the deck hardware, and moldings around the trunk cabin and toe rail. The bare underdeck should be permitted to dry in the sun. If necessary, a temporary shelter of lattice and plastic sheeting should be erected if you are in a climate where sudden rain is common. The old deck should be sanded smooth with a disc or belt sander.

Holes left from screws or bolts should be filled by dipping a dowel into WEST SYSTEM® epoxy and driving it into the hole. After the resin has set, the dowel may be cut off with a saw and filed flat with an auto-body file. Cracks in the deck or voids should be filled with a thixotropic mixture of WEST SYSTEM® epoxy and 403 microfibers in a consistency more or less like peanut butter.

The next step is to get out thin plywood panels and to fit them to the deck. The edges should slightly overlap the sheer by about ⅛ inch so that they may be planed and sanded flush with the deck. The panels should be fastened with a few screws or Monel brads to make for a perfect fit without ripples in the surface. Next, the brads are removed, a creamy-consistency WEST SYSTEM® epoxy mixture is made up, and the deck and undersurface of the plywood are saturated. The panels are fastened and the resin allowed to cure. (The directions, formulas for making mixtures, and many useful hints are available in the WEST SYSTEM® manual published by Gougeon Brothers, 706 Martin St., Bay City, MI 48706, and need not be gone into here. I am concerned with general principles rather than specific details of procedure which are better outlined in the maker's literature.)

After the new panels are cured, a choice of a final covering must be made. I think that canvas was a good choice in the days when no other fabric was available, but there are much better options today. Canvas is soft and does not resist abrasion well, it must be stitched or tacked at the seam to remain stretched, and must be painted to remain waterproof. I think that a polypropylene cloth with resin like Vectra is preferable. I consider the best covering of all to be a teakwood veneer laminated to the plywood with WEST SYSTEM® epoxy for the adhesive. This makes a fine-looking traditional deck and it is easy to fabricate from strips of about ⅛ to 3/16 inches in thickness. According to the manufacturers of WEST SYSTEM® products, strips of this thickness make the best bond, and they state that even with maintenance sanding the decks should last for twenty years in use. Seams between the teak veneers are filled with a mixture of WEST SYSTEM® epoxy and WEST SYSTEM® 423 black graphite fibers to achieve the traditional black caulked teak deck look. An advantage to veneering instead of fitting thick teak strips, as I recommended in my earlier book, is that all hardware remains in the same position and will not have to be changed.

I have tried here to outline the most practical, easiest methods for modern repairs to your boat, and I welcome comments and suggestions from my readers.

Good Sailing!

10. Fitting Out

FITTING OUT THE HULL

Whether your boat is wood, fiberglass, or metal, when the winter cover comes off you'll need a systematic procedure for getting the boat into shape for the season.

The first thing to do is choose a decent day to hose her down and give her a good scrubbing with detergent and warm water. Removing dirt and grime accumulated during storage lets you carry out a careful inspection to determine what must be done. The initial cleaning will, for example, expose hairline cracks in fiberglass gel coat, open seams and weeping fastenings in wood, and damage to the surface of metal boats.

The next step is to make an inspection list with headings for mast and rigging, deck, outside and interior of the hull. Then go over the boat inch by inch noting all defects that need repair. (Don't bother about the order of listing the jobs, by the way, because later you'll make a new work list logging repairs in order of importance and logical sequence.) Now go over the entire hull to judge the quality of the finish. In this manner you will have an accurate overview of what must be done to make the vessel ready.

FITTING OUT THE INTERIOR

If you took out all movable gear and stowed it at home last fall, then your fitting-out task will be lightened now. If you didn't, then now is the time to take life preservers and last year's canned goods out of those stuffy lockers and give everything a good airing. Bunk cushions should be placed in the sun, and given a good brushing and a shot with one of the antimildew sprays.

When everything has been removed, open up the hatches and portlights fore and aft to get a good flow of air through the hull. Mix up a bucket of warm water with a mixture of Spic and Span or one of the commercially available boat soaps and sponge the overhead, bulkheads, and cabin sole. If your boat does not have wooden drawers and other cabin furniture to warp, you can rinse off the interior with a hose. If this would spoil the interior, keep another bucket of warm water to rinse. Pay particular attention to corners where grease, dust, and dropped food particles may have gathered during last year's outings. They can cause a sour, rotted smell that invites seasickness. Next, remove the panels from the cabin sole and again do a scrub job, this time in the bilges. If enough large panels of the cabin sole are not removable, now is a good time to make them so. Take a saber saw with a stout blade and insert it into a hole drilled in the cabin floor. Saw out a portion of panel to suit you, taking care not to sever any structural members, puncture tanks, or cut electrical wires. Also, don't make the mistake of cutting through an integral structural double bottom. Through-bolt backup battens along the opening left by removing the piece and put turn-buttons alongside the adjoining pieces to keep the new access hatches in place in a seaway. Do this before you clean the bilges so that you can pump out any mess with the soapy bilgewater. Check all limber holes to be certain that they drain freely.

While the bilge is open, check plumbing that lies below the level of the cabin sole. Look at the pipes where they penetrate the skin to be certain that they are tight and there is no cracking from hull vibration. Just to be sure, give screws and bolts a turn with a wrench or screwdriver. Remove fittings that are defective and replace them. Seacocks should be checked by hand to feel if levers can be opened and closed without difficulty. If not, the apparatus should be taken apart and a small amount of water pump grease lightly smeared over the surfaces. If you find through-hull openings without proper shutoff valves, now is the time to install them.

Flush mechanisms, ballcocks, and through-hulls for marine heads, together with holding tanks and/or recirculators, should be gone over carefully and checked for proper operation. If your boat came without one, write to the manufacturer of the equipment and obtain a maintenance manual so that in the event of failure at sea you are able to make proper repairs quickly.

Freshwater and bilge pumps should be put in prime condition. If either uses leathers to maintain a pump seal, they should be taken out and lubricated so they remain soft throughout the season. Play in pump handles should be adjusted to obtain the maximum throw allowable. This will ensure lifting of the pump's full capacity of water. Hose fittings, clamps, and plumbing to the freshwater supply should be checked and repaired where necessary. Plumbing to waste outlets in the hull are especially vulnerable to slipping off or rupturing, and should be checked. Again, shutoffs should be here, readily accessible in case of emergency.

FITTING OUT FABRIC AND SAILS

Today's labor market being what it is, it pays to take first-rate care of your boat's canvas. Navy and Bimini tops, awnings, cockpit, boom, and boat covers, dodgers —everything should be hauled out at the first zephyr of spring to undergo a complete inspection.

Log each piece of canvas aboard your vessel and jot down an appraisal of its condition plus the repair work that may have to be done to put it into shape for the season. Go aboard the boat and inspect each "lift-the-dot" or stud-and-eye fastener. Many of these, when improperly anchored in the wood or fiberglass of the boat, pull out to subject tops, awning, and dodgers to unfair strain as the weight of the wind presses on the surface. Stress like this often tears the seams, grommets, or fasteners from the fabric. If the top was merely put away in the rush of decommissioning, you will find yourself with a lot of repair work to delay getting afloat. So go over canvas and sails early in the spring—the earlier the better.

If lift-the-dot fasteners have become loose, they may be laid on a piece of soft lead or brass and tapped with a plastic mallet. This will retighten the seal; do not use a metal hammer, for this may destroy the chrome plating and subject the canvas to stain from a weeping fastener. If the fabric beneath the fastener is torn, the fastener will have to be removed, the torn section cut out and a patch sewn over, and a new fastener put in.

If there are many to be replaced it might pay to buy a special setting tool, but if only a few need repair the approximate holes can be made with a razor-blade knife bearing down on a piece of wood. Stud-and-eye fasteners that are out of action will require the same treatment. Snap fasteners are a little more difficult to replace and repair, but can be done by the owner with a little care and some time spent figuring out an attack. Fasteners with moving parts can have a minute drop of very light sewing machine or mineral oil touched on them with a toothpick; wipe it off immediately in order not to stain the canvas.

If there are major repairs to be made to canvas accessories, it is best to take them all, together with a repair list and the defective parts pinned with red pieces of paper, to a professional sailmaker or canvas shop. At fitting-out time every canvas man in town will be up to his eyeballs in work, so the earlier you get your stuff there, the better your chances of getting the work done. Sometimes you can beat the racket by driving to some inland town where there is an awning maker who has the necessary tools and skills but is not swamped with boat work.

For tears along the seams that do not run for any great length, reinforcing strips can be sewn with palm and needle. If the fabric is synthetic and not too heavy, this can sometimes be done with a home sewing machine. Check with the maker of your machine for the proper needle size for heavier fabrics as this is absolutely necessary—dress needles will not do. If the seam is torn any great distance along its foot, for instance where it adjoins a coaming, the whole edge should either have the stitching removed and the piece unrolled flat or be cut off completely. A new piece of matching fabric can be sewn to overlay with the old, and a new seam marked, rubbed in, and sewn. After the patch is completed, new fasteners should be set using the cut-off piece as a pattern for correct positioning.

Navy and convertible tops with folding rod or pipe frameworks should be gone over carefully where folds and sliding brackets are positioned. These movable fittings put great strain on canvas and often pinch holes in the fabric when the tops are lowered. If the canvas bears down heavily on one of these pipe joints and is chafing, a patch should be made with the edges turned under and slipped between the fabric and the joint. It may be held there quite easily and permanently by applying a contact-type cement to both surfaces, letting it dry, and pressing home. Before affixing to the top proper, however, make a test on a piece of similar fabric as some rubberlike cements are incompatible with synthetic fabrics.

While you are looking at the rod and pipe supports, take a can of one of the marine silicone spray lubricants, slip a piece of shirt cardboard between the pipe and the fabric, and give the whole length of pipe a spray, wiping off any excess. The rods and sliders will then work smoothly when raising and lowering. Give a shot at the collapsing elbows and apply it liberally to zippers.

Synthetic fabrics are pretty much waterproof by their nature, but if your Vivitex or canvas covers drip rain in, they can be made impermeable again with a commercial waterproofer. The Astrup Co. (2937 West 25th St., Cleveland, OH 44113) and Sudbury Labs, Inc. (572 Dutton Rd., Sudbury, MA 01766), both make a waterproofing compound for marine use. Fuller Brush Co. (P.O. Box 900, Hartford, CT 06115) makes one that can also be used on lifejackets and fishing or sailing clothes. Some of these compounds have a flame-retardant and preservative quality as well.

With the modern trend to full-length camper tops in everything from sailboats to runabouts, it pays to learn something about canvas maintenance. A run through a good book on sailmaking and a chat with your sailmaker or canvas man will pay off in trouble-free boating.

Sails should be, if they haven't been already, washed in mild detergent or a commercial product especially made for sails (see the list at the end of Chapter 3) and cool water by hand—and scrubbing brush.

After the washing, they should be inspected thoroughly for rips or tears. Stitching in Dacron sails is the point of most weakness, so inspect each seam with care. Most experienced sailors make a practice of having their sailmaker examine and restitch each sail as needed every year. It is cheap and worth every penny. Home repairs are possible but usually not as satisfactory.

FITTING OUT THE RIGGING

Spars

Anodized spars can merely be washed. Nonanodized spars should be cleaned up with an abrasive (scouring powder, scouring pads, or fine wet sandpaper) and then coated with one of the clear coatings such as Sparcote formulated for this purpose. If you want a really shiny spar, buff with rubbing compound before coating. While you're cleaning, check spars for straightness, check fittings for looseness and defects (cracks in castings), and oil sheaves.

Aluminum spars are noisy, particularly with internal halyards and wiring. Wiring can be enclosed in a plastic tube or it can be seized to the after side of the spar.

Running and Standing Rigging

Running rigging should be gone over routinely not only at fitting-out time, but periodically during the season as well. Halyards take most of the strain and get heavy wear at the nip where they go around the masthead sheave in the hoist position. Wire halyards should be felt to see if there are any broken wires or excessive wear. If so, the halyard should be shortened to bring a fresh tuck over the sheave. This may involve turning in a new splice.

Rope-to-wire splices in halyards should be carefully investigated as they are a frequent source of failure. If flexible wire running rigging is fitted with swage fittings, pay special attention to junctions, which are points of particular sensitivity. Consider replacing swage fittings with more flexible splices or Nicopress fittings.

If your boat has halyard winches, they should be unrove and the wire looked at with a close eye to the point where the wire attaches to the halyard drum. Winches should be overhauled, lubricated, and tested before rewinding the wire.

If there is a spare sheave at the masthead, an extra halyard should be installed in case of failure of a main or jib halyard when underway.

Take a look at sheets for wear. Synthetics betray the beginning of deterioration when the outer circumference becomes fuzzy, gray, and dirty. If the line feels lifeless and limp, twist open the lay and take a look; it might be time to retire that one and replace it. Dead rope that has outlived its usefulness can be costly in gear failure, so don't take a chance. If the sheets are newish at the bitter end but well used at the standing part, reversing them end-for-end will often give another season's safe use. Docking lines and the dinghy painter are two other cordage items that often get overlooked and which can be expensive if they fail. Don't get into the habit of using old line for these purposes.

Standing rigging, since the advent of stainless and Monel, rarely gives trouble—especially if it gets reasonable maintenance. Whether your mast is permanently stepped or removable, get to the vangs where the heads of the shrouds are attached and check them out. Use a magnifying glass to inspect for hairline cracks. If the pins of the vangs are worn, replace them with new ones. Turnbuckles should be turned with the hand after the locknuts are loosened. If they do not turn with hand pressure, they should be freed and lubricated. A light smearing with petroleum jelly is as good as anything for this.

When adjusting the rigging, common sense is as good as a strain gauge. Just sight up the mast as you make each adjustment to be certain the stick stays straight.

Miscellaneous

Before winding up rigging, be sure to check chainplates, and bobstay and backstay fittings for wear and electrolysis. Put a squirt of silicone lubricant in the slot of the mast and boom if you do not use slides. Spruce up and lubricate the roller reefing and you'll always be able to handle stiff breezes.

Be liberal with the oil can throughout the rig. Shackles should snap, pole fittings should open easily, sheaves should revolve without strain, and track cars should move without having to be forced.

White rigging tape is a rigger's best friend. Everything that can possibly get near a sail should be taped to eliminate tearing. Additionally, when a wire is to be seized to another wire or to a piece of hardware (spreaders), tape the wire first, then seize it and follow with more tape. The first taping will effectively prevent slipping.

And don't forget the lights and instruments. Test all circuits and replace components as necessary. Check for, and replace, all corroded bulbs.

Final Word: When you're sure the rig is ready to step, look again. Now is the time to find what you forgot.

STOPPING TOPSIDE LEAKS

Leaks are a nuisance, but they can be stopped. Windshields are one of the chief offenders because their need to open prevents a permanent seal. Boatmen should carefully check the gaskets that act as water seals. New ones should be installed if the old are compressed, hardened, or crumbling. The same treatment should be given to windows and portholes of the opening type. If the dealer or manufacturer cannot supply new gaskets, a cross section of the old gasket should be taken to a marine supplier and matched as closely as possible. Old gaskets should be dug out with a screwdriver and the channel cleaned with emery paper. No adhesive is necessary if the gasket fits properly.

Most windshield closing latches and quadrant risers are inadequate. It is often impossible to exert enough force by hand to get a watertight seal. One solution is to remove factory hardware and install oversize windshield adjusters which will allow sufficient leverage.

Fiberglass boats seldom develop leaks in integrally molded sections. However, they sometimes leak around access openings such as hatches and doors. These leaks can be stopped by installation of a weatherstripping-type gasket of sponge rubber cemented in place with a rubber-base glue between the hatch rim and the hatch cover. Screw-down hatch fasteners on the underside of the hatch will pull the cover down to form a seal. Rod-type adjusters never seem to do the job as well.

Decks on fiberglass craft seldom leak, but they often do on wooden boats. Usually the biggest job is to find the leak. The best way to do this is to test a small section at a time rather than flooding the whole deck at once. A technique used in England is to build a small dam over one section at a time using plasticene or modeling clay to localize the test water. In this way you can go below to trace leaks for as long as you like. Points of greatest trouble on wooden boats are along the seam where the trunk cabin joins the deck, around hatches and deck openings, and where fittings such as mooring bitts pierce the deck. Old deck fittings that are through-bolt fastened, such as cleats, can offer a channel for leaks if the bedding compound has dried out and crumbled away. Suspect fittings should be removed, rebedded, and refastened. The Thiokol-based rubber bedding compounds or butyl rubber compounds are good for such use as they do not dry out but remain flexible.

Suspect cracks or crazes in fiberglass boats can be filled with epoxy putty, or a strip of fiberglass and resin can be laminated over the crack. Old gel coat and pigment should be roughed up with a sander to make sure of a good bond with the new lamination.

In small motor cruisers, the companionway entrance is a frequent source of leaks. It is very difficult to construct a complicated sliding/folding companion door that is really watertight. A simple solution is to make a temporary canvas dodger or cover which can be fixed with lift-the-dot fasteners for use in foul weather. The same technique can be used for especially troublesome hatches.

Small day cruisers utilize canvas and navy tops for foul-weather shelter. If properly maintained, such temporary shelters are fine. In practice, however, few boat owners give canvas superstructures proper care. Zip-on canvas covers should be inspected several times a season and the zippers should be kept lubricated with a coating of light machine oil. Snap or turn-button fastenings on the superstructure should be checked and broken ones should be replaced as soon as possible. If one or two broken fasteners are allowed to languish, when an emergency arises whole panels of navy and canvas tops cannot be secured and the top ceases to have any utility. Dot fasteners on the canvas should similarly be checked and, when torn, local reinforcing or a new square of canvas should be sewn on and a new fastener struck. If folding metal ribs are used to support the canvas over the cockpit, the canvas should be inspected for punctures where it bears on these members. A proper, dry place should be kept aboard where canvas tops are always stowed. A navy top kept in the cockpit and constantly walked over can become a sodden mess in one season.

Temporary canvas covers for ventilators, air scoops, and locker doors are a good way to keep rainwater out of the hull. Rubber stoppers and wooden plugs can be kept aboard to fill holes where engine controls and gearshift levers penetrate the hull.

One place where water must not leak is on the engine, where it can short out the wiring harness. A temporary canvas cover for the engine box is an investment in safety. A raised lip should run around the access opening to the engine compartment beneath the engine box so that rainwater in the cockpit will not enter the engine room to flood out the engine. Few boats have such a coffer dam; most rely on the engine box walls alone to keep water out. If you have the time, such a raised lip should certainly be made. Fastening to the cockpit floor should be with through-bolts and the underside of timbers should be bedded with Thiokol before fastening.

PLUMBING MAINTENANCE

Begin your fitting-out plumbing work by checking gas tanks, vents, water tanks, and fills. Gas is like dynamite in the bilge, and this check should be thorough. Twist the hose clamps, which connect the deck fill to the gas tank fill pipe, by hand using moderate pressure. If the hose or clamps turn, remove clamps, place Permatex on the joint, and replace the clamps, making sure they are tight.

Check the outboard gas vent to be sure it is not clogged. Take a look at the foundations or bedding of the fuel tanks to see whether running in heavy seas might have shifted them. Chafing here could result in a ruptured tank and disaster. Hold-downs, whether wire and turnbuckle, bolts, or strap iron, should be checked and tightened with a small wrench that is too short to apply excessive leverage. Tanks on fiberglass craft that are integral to the hull should be inspected carefully, for even built-ins have piping.

Do your work systematically. Begin aft and work forward. Engine cooling-water intake and outlets should be checked for leaks—preferably with the hull out of water and a hose attached to the system.

Corroded pipe fittings, or fittings that are still functional but have deteriorated so that a wrench slips and routine removal is impossible, should be replaced. Be sure that intake clamshells or sediment screens are clean and unobstructed. Unfortunately, too many of these fittings are installed in a way that makes routine removal and inspection of pipe fittings beneath them difficult or impossible. If screws holding clamshells have corroded heads, replace them, and check the pipe fittings while you are about it.

If you have closed-system freshwater cooling, it should be connected to a hose while the hull is on the ways and the engine should be run to check for leaks. Engine temperatures above the manufacturer's recommended limit may indicate blockage in the extreme hairpin and elbow turns that seem to be unavoidable with keel cooler piping. If this condition exists, it will be worthwhile to disassemble the unit in a systematic way till the obstruction is found. Hardware holding the cooling tubing to the hull should be carefully inspected. It is embarrassing to have a keel cooler fall off.

Engine exhaust piping should be looked at. If you have a wet exhaust, check the transom flange(s) and the hose clamps on any flexible sections in the exhaust installation. If you have a standpipe and expansion chamber in the line, as with an auxiliary, and especially if you winterized in an area with below-freezing temperatures, you should make a careful inspection of the line for ice damage. The same holds true if any type of patent wet muffler is in the line. If you have the time, the exhaust line should be wire-brushed and painted with heat-resistant paint. The line will last longer and leaks will show more clearly.

It is extremely important to have well-maintained shutoff valves in all systems. Fuel, seawater, and freshwater shutoffs are there for a reason. If they are deteriorated, corroded, or inoperative, they should be repaired or replaced. Every boatowner should know how to take apart, repair, and replace simple gate valves and globe valves. All valves should be cleaned and lubricated so that they turn easily by hand without use of pliers or pipe wrenches.

Potable water systems should be gone over carefully. After first filling, taste the water to be sure it is sweet. If it seems tainted, bacteria might be in the tanks or lines. A few water purification tablets in the tank will destroy microorganisms and give you safe, fresh water. (Try "Sweet Water" by Jasco.) Pumps in the system, whether electric or manual, should be operated and repaired where necessary. If there is undue leakage, the packing and/or washers should be replaced. If pumping is hard or has a feeling of back pressure, vent pipes may be clogged and should be reopened. Though less critical than in the fuel system, water tank foundations and hold-downs should also be inspected. If your boat has holding tanks or sumps, wherever possible the inspection plates should be removed and the tanks cleaned.

All lines from basins and sinks, especially those which discharge outboard, should be checked for leaks. Through-hull fittings especially should be looked at carefully. Wherever a seacock appears, bedding blocks and caulking should be inspected and the operating levers should be thrown back and forth to be certain they function smoothly and easily. Badly corroded or inoperative ones should be replaced (it is seldom possible or economical to repair them). If the lever merely operates with difficulty, it is possible to dismantle the apparatus and lubricate with heavy, water-resistant grease.

Machinery which operates the marine toilet aboard your craft should be checked. Hand pumps should not leak and should operate smoothly. As guests unfamiliar with the critical nature of marine toilets sometimes throw foreign matter into the bowl, this fixture always causes trouble. Human hair and/or cleanser pumice is a frequent cause of trouble, and often makes the joker or check valve inoperative with a danger of siphoning in sea water and swamping the boat. (While you are at it, now is a good time to check the legal requirements in your local waters to be certain your installation complies with regulations.)

While not "plumbing" in the usual sense, limber holes, scuppers, and self-bailing ducts from cockpits are passages through which water must pass freely. They are also passages in which dirt and debris collect most easily. Make sure they are all clear.

ORGANIZING THE STOWAGE

When your boat is all ready to receive her gear, don't just jam everything aboard haphazardly. Lay everything out on a garage floor and divide it by "departments." Put bosun's stores, ropes, anchor chain, etc., in one place, engine stores somewhere else, and galley equipment in a third location. Next, make an inventory listing each item and note the place where it is stowed on the master-plan. During the season this will prove a boon if you're trying to find the spare stove parts, for instance, in choppy weather with half a dozen guests aboard. If you have to change location of any item for any reason, be sure to make a correction on the inventory. The inventory can be kept in a plastic envelope in some handy spot.

ALUMINUM BOATS

Unless it is painted or anodized, aluminum protects itself from deterioration by forming a thin film of aluminum oxide in contact with the air. For an unpainted boat, usually a good washing with an Oakite or Spic and Span solution in hot water will remove crusted salt, "white rust" oxidation, and grime. A cleaner-polisher specially formulated for aluminum is available at most hardware and marine specialty stores and works well, after which a coat of clear carnauba wax should be applied.

Bare aluminum boats require an etching solution to give a "tooth" or anchor to the surface so that the prime and finish coats adhere. All major paint companies make such solutions and also offer compatible prime and finish paints. The best way to go about painting an unpainted aluminum boat is to look over the literature in your dealer's display, discuss the options with him or the foreman of the paint shop, and then follow directions. If the hull has already been painted, usually a light sanding with a fine production or wet-or-dry sand paper and direct application right over the old paint is possible. Be sure to wash well, however, and some of the solvent to be used for the chosen paint can be used to moisten a rag to wipe off grease and tar.

Stern-drive and outboard motor units are made of aluminum too, and must be prepared and treated for painting in the same manner as any other aluminum in contact with water, except that it is advisable to build up extra coats. Special self-spraying lacquer enamel for above the waterline is available as well as lower-unit lacquer enamel and antifouling in spray cans.

STEEL BOATS

Seldom, if ever, will a boat owner have to undertake the complete painting of a bare steel hull, as this is generally a task for the professional. Maintenance of existing coatings and repairs to areas damaged by grounding or impact, plus first coating of minor additions, is about the most that the owner will ever be called upon to do. Steel, contrary to general opinion, will last a respectably long time if it is properly painted and maintained.

In order for steel to last, besides the primer coats that seal the prepared metal from the air, a water-impermeable barrier coat is applied. This barrier is designed to keep the water from ever touching the metal plating, and, to prevent electrolysis, is usually built up from several coats of bituminoid-base material. After the barrier has been applied, a finish coat, usually vinyl base, and then an antifouling paint are laid on. Above the waterline the procedure is essentially the same except that additional finish coats instead of antifouling are used.

When there has been breakdown of steel hull topsides paint, the affected area should be lightly touched with a disc sander or powered wire brush to bring the patch back to clean, rustless metal. Several coats of primer should be applied to protect the bare metal and to build up the indentation left by cleaning so it is even with the rest of the hull. Red lead, zinc chromate, and several of the especially prepared commercial mixes make good primers. Next, one or more coats are applied followed by either finish or antifouling, depending on whether it's an underwater or a topsides area. If the indentation left by brushing or grinding is of considerable depth, an epoxy-base metal-filling compound similar to that used in auto work should be used to level the void. After filling, the painting procedure is followed.

Other underwater iron and steel such as centerboards, chainplates, pintles and gudgeons, keels, etc., should be treated in like manner. A trouble area is often the interior surface of ironwork fastened to the hull, such as chainplates. Sometimes, especially if there is considerable rusty weeping, it will pay to take off these fittings, remove the rust to bright metal, paint them, and replace with an elastomeric sealant gasket behind them. When replacing, be careful to use fastenings of the same metal to avoid galvanic corrosion due to electrolytic action of dissimilar metals.

TOOLS FOR TUNING AND SPRUCING UP

While it's true that earlier skippers got by well enough with a little fire and a sharp stone adze when they wanted to hollow out a log, today's sailor is really in luck. There are tools available this year that can make a boat owner feel like he is an experienced shipwright. Some new implements make hard jobs easy. Others simply save hours of time.

Choice of tools is a personal matter, but there should be little argument about buying the best. A wrench with jaws not quite wide enough or a cheap screwdriver that breaks when you try to use the shaft to open a shackle can be an annoyance ashore but sometimes a disaster afloat. And since few of us work full time at boat maintenance, we may not use a dull or makeshift implement with skill.

Probably the simplest tool kit is the leather sheath strapped on by the offshore sailor. Its knife, fid, and pliers with a small adjustable crescent wrench on the end of one handle and screwdriver on the other can take care of many chores and emergencies. (Note that it is worn in back so that a fall will not push the knife or marlin spike into your leg.) Add a Swiss army knife, with its remarkable saw and scissors, in another pocket and you have the essentials for cruising on someone else's boat.

For fitting-out use ashore and later aboard your boat, be sure to have the following:

Basic Ashore-and-Afloat Tool Kit

Hammer	Screwdriver
Knife	Chisel
Pliers	Drill and bits
Adjustable wrench	

These can be sprayed with some rust inhibitor like GE's Silicone Lubricant and stowed in a plastic tool box or rolled up in West Marine Products' tie-on rigger's apron or tool bag.

Maintenance Tools for Boat Owners
Depending on other factors—such as whether a boat is power or sail, large or small, day runabout or offshore cruiser, outboard or inboard, cold-weather cabin job or open utility for the tropics—the choice of essentials for the complete fitting-out tool set (with the exception of power tools) might include these listed below:

Basic Afloat-Ashore Kit plus:

Cross-cut saw
Hacksaw
Brace with bits up to 1″
　dia.
Set of screwdrivers with
　insulated handles, large
　models with square
　shafts
Chisels, ½″ and 1″
Oval rasp
Assorted files
Set of open-end wrenches
　(in both inch and

metric measures)
Adjustable plumber's
　wrench
Needle and snubnose
　pliers
Metal snips
Plane
Plug cutter
Vise-grip pliers
Yankee screwdriver with
　regular and
　phillips-head bits
Plus your own favorites

The use for most of these is obvious. Backing out corroded screws seems to be a continual chore, and a brace fitted with a screwdriver bit, a hollow-plug cutter to remove the wood around an imbedded screw or bolt, or a large square-shafted screwdriver to which a wrench may be fitted are all useful.

Power tools, of course, are the real boon to the pleasure boater. Remember twenty years ago when a power hand drill was a machine shop or boatyard tool that few amateurs owned? For occasional use the ¼-inch model is satisfactory, but a ⅜-inch drill is better for continuous work—not because the added ⅛ inch is so valuable but because the larger size is usually built for much heavier duty work.

In case you haven't looked recently, note the variety of hand-drill accessories now available, as listed below. Attachments provide the push for everything from right-angle screwdrivers to clamp-on sanders and saber saws. Or a simple router bit can be chucked in for keyhole cuts.

Want to use ½-inch drills in a ¼-inch chuck? There's a choice between an accessory oversize chuck or shanked-down bits. Pleasure boaters have recently been tempted by disc, belt, and orbital power sanders. This year the innovations are in saws that can handle boating problems. A new Rockwell 314 trim saw is designed to cut through plastic laminates such as fiberglass, plus plywood, thin nonferrous metals, Plexiglas, and other materials up to 1 1/16″ thick. A tilt base provides angles up to 45°, while a slip clutch guards against kickback. Boatlife also has a deck and hull saw reported to trim fiberglass, rout seams, and operate forward or backward, left- or right-handed, with a reversible motor and two-way blade.

Power to the Pleasure Boater
Tools include:

    Paint remover heaters
    Shop vacuum cleaners
    Soldering guns and irons
    Disc, belt, and orbital sanders
    Circular and saber saws
    Hand drills—with accessories such as: router and expansion bits, screwdriver, angle and speed reduction heads with slip clutch, drill press, oversize chucks and bits, water pump

Since a boat is often bound to be near water, it is important that power tools be well insulated, that three-wire extension cords be used, and that tools have three-prong plugs to ground the device and prevent serious shocks. One alternative is to find a self-powered hand drill that is charged in advance and can also be used offshore, away from power line connections. Double-insulated tools also reduce shock hazard. Boatyards beat the shock hazard problem with air-powered pneumatic tools, but they are too expensive for once-a-year use by the amateur shipwright.

In addition to tools, a lot of other items seem to end up in the tool locker as well. A piece of canvas or tarpaulin, for instance, can be spread out in the cockpit or on the ground in a boatyard to keep a greasy pump you're working on from dirtying the deck. Here are other items that are useful:

Nontools for Your Tool Box

Oil can   Fid   Whetstone
Tarpaulin   Magnet   Flashlight
Tape   Whipping thread   Rags
Plastic drop cloth   Monel wire
Rigger's apron   Roll of paper towels
Staple gun and Monel staples
Can of silicone lubricant
Can of bedding and sealing compound
Epoxy putty and glue   Marline
Stainless-steel cotter rings and pins
Stainless shackles and hose clamps
Trouble lamp and extension cord
Current checker and continuity tester
Pencils   Pad   Tape measure

CHECKLISTS FOR FITTING OUT

☐ Assorted production sandpaper
☐ Batteries and case
☐ Bolts, screws, nails
☐ Brush cleaners
☐ Degreaser: engine and general
☐ Drop light

☐ Dust pan and brush
☐ Engine tools: inboard and outboard
☐ Extension cord
☐ Fasteners
☐ Fiberglass repair kit
☐ Fire extinguisher
☐ Grease

☐ Hose clamps
☐ Hose and nozzle
☐ Hull detergents
☐ Lubricants
☐ Lumber
☐ Mildew preventive
☐ Mop and bucket
☐ Nails
☐ Paint: bottom, topsides, deck, engine, accessories
☐ Paint remover
☐ Pipe fittings
☐ Polishes, fiberglass hull and metal
☐ Power sander
☐ Preservatives
☐ Rags
☐ Razor blades
☐ Repair parts: engine, inboard and outboard

☐ Respirator
☐ Rigging tools
☐ Sacrificial zincs
☐ Sail fabric
☐ Sail repair tools
☐ Sanitation equipment parts
☐ Scraper and blades
☐ Scrub brush
☐ Seam compound and sealants
☐ Sponges
☐ Tack rag and dust brush
☐ Tape: masking, electrical, sail repair
☐ Thinners and solvents
☐ Vacuum cleaner
☐ Window-washing liquid
☐ Woodworking tools
☐ Wire

☐ Battery
☐ Bilge pumps
☐ Blower systems
☐ Caulking
☐ Check fastenings for weeping
☐ Check for soft planks
☐ Cooling-water intake strainers
☐ Crankcase oil
☐ Dinghy
☐ Docklines
☐ Engine controls
☐ Electronic equipment
☐ Engine wiring harness
☐ Fill hull gouges

☐ Fire extinguishers
☐ Flush and rinse water tanks
☐ Free seacocks
☐ Freshwater pumps
☐ Fuel filter bowl
☐ Fuel tanks
☐ Fuses
☐ Ground tackle
☐ Icebox
☐ Inspect for electrolysis
☐ Install sacrificial zincs
☐ Install and swing compass
☐ Inventory gear
☐ Keel bolts

- [ ] Lifesaving equipment
- [ ] Make defect list
- [ ] Make stowage list
- [ ] Marine head
- [ ] Oil in the reduction gear
- [ ] Oil strainer
- [ ] Overhaul running rigging
- [ ] Paint
- [ ] Ports and windows
- [ ] Prime filled spots
- [ ] Propeller gland nuts, strut bearings
- [ ] Refrigeration
- [ ] Repack stuffing box
- [ ] Rode
- [ ] Rudder hardware
- [ ] Sand prime keel
- [ ] Scrape, sand, prime fill seams
- [ ] Scrub and wash hull
- [ ] Scuppers
- [ ] Shaft alignment
- [ ] Standing rigging
- [ ] Steering controls
- [ ] Stove
- [ ] Wash, inspect sails
- [ ] Wash, polish, wax fiberglass
- [ ] Winches

Index